Robin T. Smith

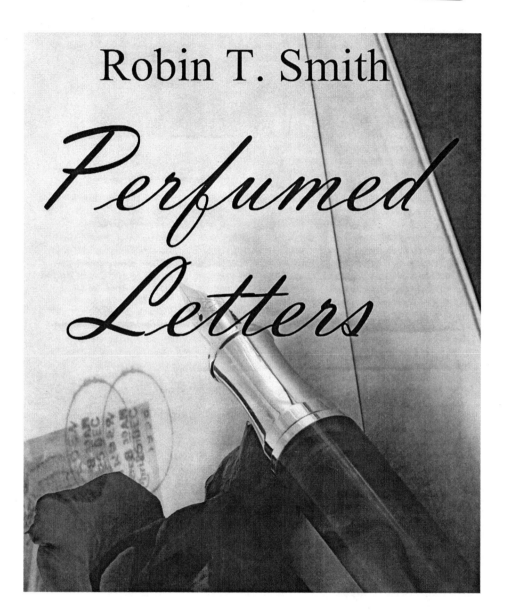

Perfumed Letters

outskirtspress
DENVER, COLORADO

Table of Contents

In order to gain clarity and a better understanding of the knowledge and wisdom breathed upon this word, we must lay the foundation. Let's pray:

Father, in the name of Jesus, we come to You acknowledging who You are in our lives as King, Restorer, and Deliverer. Holy Spirit, comfort us and guide us in all truth. Open and enlighten our hearts that we may receive, our minds that we may understand, and our spirits so we may be transformed to glorify You. I decree and declare the message written in this book blessed as You fill our hearts with wisdom, encouragement, and strength. By the blood of Jesus, I dismantle any and all plans of the enemy to uproot this word from our lives. I pray this word will permeate in our spirit for a fresh revelation needed right now. I give You all my praise and thanks, because we decree and declare it is already done. In Jesus' name, amen.

Introduction

"Perfume delights the heart...." (Proverbs 27:9)

There isn't a woman on earth who does not have a perfume or fragrance that makes her feel clean, beautiful, and sexy. It is an extension, a mirrored reflection of who we are. Perfume, whether in liquid form or when found in powder or clay cosmetics, has been around since ancient Egypt, from its main use of pleasing pagan gods to religious burials. Perfume thereafter was not worn simply to mask an odor; it was coveted, and considered a symbol of economic and social status. This costly fragrance was a luxury reserved for the wealthy and noble among kings and queens for usage on special occasions, and as a commodity. It was used by physicians for medicinal practices and by priests for religious ceremonial purposes.

Today, perfume is more of a necessity than a luxury. Perfumes and fragrances are not worn only for celebrations such as weddings and graduations, but are part of our everyday living, found in deodorants, lotions, and body washes, to car fresheners and household products like dryer sheets and kitchen cleaners. What kind of condition would our world be in without it? It would be much like a world without color: absolute boredom.

Why are we drawn to fragrance? What makes scent so important? Is the sense of smell as vital to us as sight, taste, touch, and hearing? Our sense of smell is imperative for many reasons. Scientific research has suggested that smell transmits messages directly to the section of the right brain that determines emotional response and behavior. It powerfully invokes short-term and long-term memory from certain experiences; it influences sexuality; and its sensitivity assists in protecting us from harm. From a spiritual and natural perspective, our sense of smell is a gift of discernment.

Chocolate. Pizza. The hair salon. Cigarette smoke. Baby lotion. Fried chicken. Orange zest. Spoiled milk. Freshly cut grass. The gym. From pleasant and unpleasant odors alike, we can discern what objects are prior to physically seeing them. Fragrance is not something we can see on a person. Nobody walks around with a Chanel No. 5 box on their neck or a mini tester strapped to their wrist, but you can smell the perfume. Our sense of smell can instantaneously take us back to a moment of time; recalling the season, a specific event, people, and what was done or said, easily arousing emotions that may have been suppressed in our subconscious.

What is that one scent that will take you back to a flood of memories of *ooh la la* and other happy thoughts? My mother used to wear a perfume called Sun, Moon, and Stars by Karl Lagerfeld. The bottle is embellished in a frosty midnight blue, covered in imprints of stars with a circular gold-stained top. The fragrance is modestly soft, warm, and inviting, with a hint of jazz. It is classy and graceful, like the beautiful woman my momma has become. The perfume itself did not define her, but rather enhanced the feminine attributes of lady, wife, mother, and friend, engaging me into the totality of a woman's essence. This scent alone evokes many memories of my mother getting ready for church, among other outings.

More captivating than the perfume my mother wore are the spiritual fragrances she has been wearing since the day she encountered Jesus, accepting Him as her Lord and Savior. On good days in glory to fierce battle fronts and admirable humility in between, by my mother's remarkable scent savvy, I witnessed first-hand how the anointed fragrances of Christ are refreshing and altogether lovely. Despite my detestable attitude as a teenager and trying-to-find-myself as a young adult, because of the fragrances of Christ that I was trained up in, when I became older I did not depart from them and I was compelled to be drawn by the fragrant aromas of Christ.

Where would we be without the signature fragrances of Christ in our lives? Where would we be without a sound mind, love, humility, or the heavenly scents of worship and prayer? If those are signature fragrances, what makes our perfume the most splendid of all? Dear Royal Heiress, as we engage in the conversation, sit back and relax. Our Father has given you a signature fragrance and a perfume especially made for you. You are softly perfumed in the love of His Spirit. You are written in His heart…you are God's Perfumed Letter.

Heaven's Perfumery

"The heavens declare the glory of God; the skies proclaim the work of His hands." (Psalm 19:1)

Every good and perfect gift comes from above, and I would like to introduce you to Heaven's Perfumery where the best-selling perfumes and fragrances are created, developed, and refined. What is perfume? Merriam-Webster's dictionary defines perfume as "a substance that emits a pleasant odor." Perfume derives from the Hebrew word "qe-toreth" (pronounced ket-o'-reth) meaning smoke, odor of (burning) sacrifice, incense; but it also has origins in the Latin root words "per" meaning through or with, and "fumar," meaning to smoke. We can begin our aromatherapy journey knowing that according to God, only through the smoke will the scent of something pleasant or sweet come forth.

In order for any vision or goal to take flight, one has to begin with the end in mind. A vision and purpose must be established. God, as our Perfumer and Chief Executive Officer of Heaven's Perfumery, is a connoisseur of perfume and has, historically, a deep eternal passion for sweet-smelling fragrances. There are hundreds of mentions in the Bible with reference to fragrance, scents, and perfume respectively, including but not limited to cinnamon, myrrh, aloe, hyssop, fragrant oil, frankincense, etc. Beginning as flowers of God, each of us has a unique fragrance that delights Him. As the Author and Finisher of your faith, every detail from ingredients used and composition in which your perfume is created, is carefully fashioned and complimentary with His love.

The Perfumer is the same yesterday, today and forever. His methodologies and formulas have not changed--only the faces of the women chosen to wear the perfume. He remains in the highly lucrative business of creating special fragrant aromas for daughters of the Royal Priesthood. Before you were born, nestled in your mother's womb, God knew you before the foundation of the world. (Jeremiah 1:5) He knew the purpose for which you were to be created, where you would be intended for use and the chronological appointed time to do the work to glorify Him.

Allow me to clarify for the ladies who are reverting back to the word "use." You are not here for yourself. I am all for independence and I'm not debasing it at all. However, I am relating two simple messages in this book. One, God put you here on Earth to be a blessing to someone else. This is not about you. You must recognize that the Perfumer develops a scented fragrance product which is designed specifically for you and or through you to be a blessing to another person. Two, you are the righteousness of God, and that right standing is not a feeling, but a certified and true fact of a Perfumed Letter.

What is the difference between a perfume and a fragrance? Spiritually speaking, your perfume is your anointing. It is your oil. It is the divine purpose for which God created you on this earth. It is the blanketing of God's super on your natural God-given talent or gift for the advancement of the kingdom. With that, you can understand you don't have to work for your perfume, knowing it is a gift everything else you need and desire in this existence—resources, finances, power, etc.--are released in your perfume. The fragrances are divine tools used to equip and support your perfume to aid in the release of your oil.

Before the process begins, God, Jesus, and the Holy Spirit consult during a board meeting about the fragrance that will be custom-designed for you. The Perfumer (God) is briefed on purpose (your anointing), composition (personality of mind, heart, and soul), and ingredients (life-altering events, situations, and challenges) that will be used as weight to press out your oil. All three contain the blueprint of your life, but are not all-inclusive regarding the circumstances surrounding your birth, family placement, ethnicity, temperament, eye color, body silhouette, talents, gifts, etc. Once the criteria are met and a decision has been finalized (Psalm 119:89), the flowers are then chosen.

Flowers and other plants are the root and origin of all perfumes, be they synthetic or authentic. Jesus, an excellent vinedresser aptly known as the Lily of the Valley will, at the appointed time, walk along heaven's garden beds, choosing flowers that have been pruned who are ready and available for the laborious developmental process, which takes place at the Garden of Gethsemane.

The Garden

Why the Garden of Gethsemane? It is a place of pressure and pressing. It is Hebrew for "oil press." Merriam-Webster's dictionary defines Gethsemane as "a place or occasion of great mental or spiritual suffering." From the moment of conception through our birth until today, we have been pushing and pressing in this garden. It is a place where spiritual character is polished and faith is strengthened. We spend the majority of our spiritual lives' blood, sweat, or tears transitioning out of or in Gethsemane. The garden is a key place in the arduous development and refinement of a perfume and a fragrance unique to us. Here, we are pulled from our stems and our petals are plucked from their center. At this point, we are taken to the rock to be pounded and crushed. (2 Corinthians 4: 8-10) The book of Hosea, Chapter 6:1-2, summarizes the Garden this way:

Come, and let us return to the Lord.
For He has torn but He will heal us.
He has stricken, but He will bind us up.
After two days He will revive us.
On the third day He will raise us up that we may live in His sight.

The compressing of your petals is simply God using the weight of ingredients—those circumstances and life events--to press out your oil. (Romans 5:3) It is obviously inevitable that this is a place of pain and tears. Your pain may be penetrating the very core of your being, but the pressing of your life's petals is the key to creating the oil of a sweet-smelling fragrance that fills His nostrils. I know it sounds harsh, but this is the place where we get knowledgeable and real about our true character--not one of a precarious nature by society. It is in this garden, we are reacquainted with Christ not just for what He does, but for the essence and power of who He is. And because we worship Him in spirit and in truth, we recognize that it is not the garden itself that is pressing; it is our spiritual mindset about the garden. How you perceive the situation, circumstance, or event--before, during, and after-- also determines how much oil will be pressed out.

Let's recall when Jesus visited this garden. See Matthew 26: 36-56.

One, we find that although Jesus came to the garden of Gethsemane with his boys, He did not go into this garden with his team. He entered in alone. There are just some tests and trials in which neither your girls nor your BFF or Grandmomma's prayer will be able to go with you. You will have to go to God and seek Him for yourself. The weight Jesus was feeling was nearly unbearable and yours will be no different. This was all God, and yet all man, saying "Let this cup pass from me." (Luke 22:42) I know we can all relate. God, do I really have to go through this... right now? The pain can be so excruciating; one may look to pills, out of control shopping, sex, and even suicide. But believers, don't faint in the day of adversity. Our response, no matter how pressing, should be like Jesus: "Lord, have your way" --and mean it.

Two, after the betrayal and His arrest, Jesus had a member of his crew who was "ride or die," and that individual assaulted one of the soldiers for coming at Jesus wrong. Jesus had to remind his friend of who He was and His access to power. He told him, "You don't think I can call a hood of angels to handle business?" Three, He had to let him know, it is what it is. He told him this had to be done because if the scriptures were not fulfilled, Destiny would have nowhere to turn after the miscarriage. "If I don't go through this I won't be able to restore Malaysia into the great woman God called her to be after being taken advantage of by so many men, or be Stephanie's peace, when she has to deploy, leaving her two children behind. I have to go through this in order to be a deliverer for Angela when she when calls on me because the doctor is going to tell her in year xxxx, she has stage two breast cancer. I did not go through all this for Me. I had to go through to fulfill the scriptures so My daughters who are reading this book will know I am their God, I love them, and they are my special treasure, my Perfumed Letters."

The Garden of Gethsemane is not necessarily a bad place, although it may feel like a living hell. We have to go through it to press out the oil for our perfume. Within this oil is a source of deliverance, hope, and inspiration that will loosen and break chains, and remove impossibility, dismantling all plans of the enemy. We have to go through, for it is the answer to someone else's prayer.

Upon going through, yes going through (Psalm 23:4) this compression, we have the tendency to get mad at God, doubt our faith, and feel burdened. We have thoughts of: God, I can't take any more of this, this is some BS, or we feel like quitting. Remember, ladies, God is already at end of your story. He's waiting right there at the "happily ever after." Happily ever after, my butt! Yes, I hear you. Seriously, God promises a wonderful ending of your life's story. Happily ever after is real. It's not just a Disney thing. (2 Corinthians 2:14)

Which of the following is your state of compression? Okay, it's been two years, five months, one week, and three days since you had but sex (but who's counting); been on the job eight years and this new chic comes in and gets the promotion; my kid is sick and the other just can't seem to stay out of trouble; recently divorced; my rent is past due; I ain't got no money for gas or a bus pass; my check is being garnished; I am thinking about an abortion; my car has broken down AGAIN; the child support isn't enough; invested all my time, love, and money to that sorry excuse for a man (whom I still love--why, I don't know) who ended up getting engaged to another; my momma is ill--the cancer has exacerbated; my daughter is pregnant (oh, and I'm on the "board"); I am so close to getting this degree; if my boss says one more thing to me, God it's a promise he'll see law before grace in my "pre-Christian" day.

There is a list of myriad circumstances and situations that could apply to any one of us. Believe this: He loves you. He has all power in His hands. God cannot lie and will not go back on His word...unlike some people. He said He wouldn't put more on you than you can bear. He said in Jeremiah 29:11 that He knows the plans He has for you--plans to prosper you, not to harm you, to give you hope and a future. In spite of all the pressing, do you believe that is the question?

I understand how crazy it can be sometimes, trying to believe and trust in what you cannot see after having been lied to by the world and taken advantage of for so long, but as believers, we walk this out by faith. I need for you to understand that the compression is working out for your good. (Romans 8:28) What if you feel you aren't there yet? I'm not trying to be rude. One, this not about your feelings. Two, I will give you five minutes after the end of this sentence to cry, scream, yell, throw some punches at a pillow, or break a glass that you don't mind replacing. Go on cry if you need to, because when we cry out to God, He is remembering His covenant with you. With every tear, He is remembering His promises to you. (Exodus 2: 23-24) Take as much time as you need. I'll be right here when you get back.

Satan is out to rape you for everything you have, steal anything attached to you, and kill all the dreams and desires you can conceive--oh, and of course, destroy your existence. This is not a game. His mission is to take you out by any means necessary. Your objective is to be proactive, and not reactive: Find out who God is in order to know who you are. This cannot happen by purchasing a necklace with a cross it or imitating a celebrity. I can take it one step further. You will not find out who God is by believing every word of a preacher alone. Yes, for every reference to scripture verbal or written, verify that is indeed true. Get a Bible and read it. The Word of God tells us you to study to show yourself approved. If you make the effort, God will do the rest.

Until I began the diligent search to find out who I was in Christ, I did not know my name and kept wondering why I was losing a battle that has already been won. (Ecclesiastes 3:15) When you figure out who God really is, you will know exactly who you are, not giving thought to society's evaluation of you. If you don't know your history, you will never know your name. If you don't know your Father, a void will forever remain, whether it is acknowledged or not...and you will find something or someone to try to fill that void. His word says: For if he has set eternity in the hearts of men (Ecclesiastes 3:11), thus He has already put a portion of Himself in your soul. No amount of designer brands, money, orgasms, degrees, or anything else can fill that void.

Please know that while the crushing and pounding of your petals is hurting, it's all worth it. (2 Corinthians 4:8) Well, what if you feel like it's just not worth the effort to continue? You did not get saved to quit. Maybe you have prayed and the circumstances have not changed—yet. Get an attitude like James, and count it all joy. (James 1:2) I know you're saying, "Yeah, right-- this chic has lost her mind." Hear me out first. I know it doesn't feel like it or look like it, but God knows exactly what He is doing. Trust Him.

Extraction

There are many methods by which to extract the oil for your perfume, but I want to focus on these three: distillation, expression, and cold pressing. Extraction is a method that immediately pulls pure concentration from the flower's raw material. When God extracts the oil out of you needed for your perfume, He is pulling out of Himself, just like He did when He created you, saying: Let Us make man in Our image. One specific mention of God in doing this is when He pulled oil out of Himself, using His Son, Jesus (John 3:16 and Acts 10:38) As part of your salvation, the same oil of Jesus—His anointing--breaks yokes, delivers, and redeems. God takes the extraction process seriously, and there will not be anything added or taken from the formula without His permission. Jesus has an established patent and firm copyright on every perfume. Neither will the oil's ingredients or composition be reproduced (Exodus 30: 32-33), as all rights were reserved at the cross. No matter what extraction method is used, it is for your good.

Distillation

Distillation is a process that uses steam. According to the Internal Journal of Comprehensive Pharmacy, "boiling begins when the sum of the partial pressures of the two immiscible liquids... [*between the flesh and the spirit*]...exceeds the atmospheric pressure..[*so that*]...the "compounds...can be purified." Italics mine. In this process flowers are laid out, placed upon a rock altar for boiling in the furnace of affliction, and steam passes through them. As the steam passes through the flower, a small proportion of scent is released. As the steam and scent are cooled (as a prayer is answered or deliverance has come) the fragranced oil rises from within the pressed flower petals.

Distillation is the seemingly never-ending fight with your old self versus the new self, losing your life in order to gain it. This process is infused with pressurized steam to bring the flesh under subjection, also known as working out your own salvation. It is being deliberately placed into a situation in which you have to choose to press forward, when going backward for just a moment would be so much easier--and the relief, a guilty pleasure. Paul explains in Philippians 3:7-9, NIV: But whatever was to my profit I now consider loss for the sake of Christ. What is more, I consider everything a loss compared to the surpassing greatness of knowing Christ Jesus my Lord, for whose sake I have lost all things. I consider them rubbish, that I may gain Christ and be found in Him, not having a righteousness of my own that comes from the law, but that which is through faith in Christ—the righteousness that comes from God and is by faith.

Paraphrasing what he said: *You're right, I could have cussed you out and probably had a right to, and I know it would have made me feel better, but I'm not there anymore, for the relationship of knowing Jesus. It's not worth it; Christ means more to me than this. With the old me, it was to my benefit to exert energy arguing with you, or opt for revenge after being taken advantage of. However, the new me in the righteousness of God by faith, knows who I am and my worth. I'll pray for you instead.*

Although the heat may be turned up to a boil with certain issues you will be faced with, know that He who is in you is greater than he who is in the world. There are some things that God will provide a way of escape for, while others it's a fact of how badly you want your blessing. God is there for you, and the Holy Spirit can lead you and guide you, but it's a matter of choice. Will the new you run it and release a fragrant oil, or will you choose to allow your old self to be the boss?

Expression

Expression is a method that does not use heat, only immersion in water. The Internal Journal of Comprehensive Pharmacy suggests after absorption in water, the plant is turned upside down, creating elasticity that aids in opening oil cells. It is held within a sponge and then squeezed to release the oil. When the sponge becomes saturated with volatile oil, it is collected in a vessel.

The process of expression can be perceived as those events in our lives that take us by surprise and stretch our faith, uprooting us from complacency and the mindset of limiting God. It is trusting Jesus to provide when you have more bills than money, and to allow Him to heal your broken heart after having been ravished repeatedly. It's believing the Holy Spirit to be your counselor, leading and guiding you when confusion sets in, questioning whether you made the right choice.

Expression is a method of extraction used when your world literally turns upside down and you have no choice but to immerse yourself in the refuge of Him (Psalm 46:1), taking faith and trusting Him when hurricanes come after beautiful weekends and earthquakes shake all in your life to its core. When a situation of this magnitude occurs, it climaxes well beyond your comfort zone. You know you cannot tweak this one. You know you don't have the resources or finances to help you pull a miracle all your own. This can be done only by the hand of God. It's a clear sign that God wants to be pleased with your faith. The elasticity of faith will stretch you to believe without a doubt He is the Great I AM and release a pleasingly fragrant oil as a ready vessel.

Cold Pressing

Cold pressing is a method of low-heat extraction, being pressed with the stone, the chief cornerstone. This process is varied with the lightest pressures specific to the individual, by puncturing the rind or peel of the plant, to obtain just enough oil to continue the flow for a specific purpose needed to release your perfume or fragrance. An example of cold pressing would be those pet peeves we have that irritate and annoy us that snap our peace or joy for literally a minute. Each time the opportunity of this small cold press presents itself by igniting a tiny flare within and we choose not to give in or blow it out of proportion, we release a little more of our oil.

I think I am cold pressed every time I drive. I have an issue with people who don't know how to drive. I mean not using turn signals, pumping brakes right as they pass the cop, or not judging speed of vehicles already on the highway correctly when merging, or in the fast lane going about 45 miles per hour. Oh, those instances can get on my last nerve! However, I am learning to check myself to be content in every state, not allowing anyone or anything to steal my joy. I have noticed that when I do this, I am actually happier and a bit more relaxed. Mind you, this is a work in progress....

Assuredly, in the light of any method, one can see that hurt and pain in some fashion are not always avoidable. We may question with tears and a heavy heart, "Why is this happening? God has left me. He has forgotten about me." In the book of Isaiah 54:7-8, NKJV provides us with some clarity. It reads:

7:    "For a mere moment I have forsaken you, but with great mercies I will gather you.

8:      with a little wrath I hid My face from you for a moment: But
        with everlasting kindness, I will have mercy on you," says
        the Lord, your Redeemer.

In verse seven "moment" is the situation, circumstance, or challenge we find ourselves in. The word forsaken comes from the Hebrew word "azab," defined as "to let go" or "allow to leave" in Vine's Concise Dictionary. It does not necessarily mean abandon within this context, but to let go temporarily. Our Lord has told you: "Lo, I am with you always even until the ends of the earth," so He will never leave you. We do not abandon our children when they are learning to ride a bike. We simply let go for a moment. Continuing on to verse eight, "with a little wrath I hid My face from you for a moment"; God may have to light a fire underneath our butts during developing or refinement to get us to where we need to be. At other times, this may be due to our having deliberately disobeyed Him. He is righteous as He is love, and will not be mocked. It is of no consequence that we are going to reap what we sow.

To my knowledge in my walk with Christ, there are only two times in which God has "forsaken" or turned His face from His children on an occasion of pressing. The first happened to Samson after he reluctantly told Delilah the source of his strength; and the other happened when Jesus was crucified at the cross. Like any parent, it hurts to see your children hurt and even angry when they are disobedient. I remember growing up in a household where my mom didn't spare *any* rods. At the appointed time to drive out any foolishness, she would say, "This is going to hurt me more than it's going to hurt you." OMG, I thought, you've got to be kidding me--you are not the one getting a whupping. Other times, she let me fall on my face. In her mind, because she loved me, she had to "let go" and let God, allowing the word to intervene with that belt.

After the pressing and extraction are processed in the Garden of Gethsemane, your perfume is ready for the Lord's use. However, there are a few stages that you should understand about the way a perfume's concentration works. Take a look at the below pyramid. From top to bottom the flow of concentration would be the Holy Spirit, Jesus, and God categorized into three stages: top, middle, and base notes. All three (1 John 5:7) combined are one known as an accord, or the harmony that makes up the basis of your perfume.

Holy Spirit

Top Note

Jesus

(Heart/Middle Note)

God

(Base Note)

Top notes are light in fragrance, and are considered the first impression. The concentration on this level is Comforter, Counselor, and Guide. The top notes are your initial attraction to a perfume, which will prompt or dismiss your choice to accept and buy the perfume.

We become ambassadors of Christ when we accept Jesus into our hearts, which means you represent something greater than yourself. One of the privileges of being in the Royal Priesthood is having the evidence of speaking in tongues, and the Holy Spirit becomes our guide. As an ambassador of Christ, the Holy Spirit--light and airy-- is what initially attracts people to the Christ in us. He's usually very subtle and soft in approach. This note attracts people with the "Oh, it's just something about her" thoughts, or "I don't know what it is, but I am intrigued and would like to know more."

The middle note--or heart note, as it is called--is Jesus. As the top note dissipates, He makes room for our Lord. One is led to the heart of the perfume, the core and the center of who we are: Jesus. Jesus then draws you by His truth and love, knocking at the door of your heart, accepting all of your imperfections, offering you a forever forgiveness, an unconditional love man knows not of. The heart of a perfume is what gives it fullness, commanding your attention, captivating us to want more. This fullness is Jesus, in salvation, redemption and righteousness of God. When you allow Him to enter in, you find that He is the missing piece that fills the void.

After the Holy Spirit whispers and Jesus knocks at the door of your heart from his heart and you accept, we are greeted with base notes. The base notes are the depth and foundation of any perfume. Concentration: love and power. As the Creator and Sustainer of life, He ultimately determines how long your aroma will last. Consequently, as Omnipresent, Omnipotent, and Omniscient, He is the most potent, concentrated version of your perfume. The closer you get to Him, the sweeter your scent will become.

Reflection: In Mark 10:45, the Bible says: "For the Son of Man did not come to be served, but to serve, and to give his life as a ransom for many." Inside Heaven's Perfumery and the Garden of Gethsemane, the pressing and extraction have a purpose. The purpose in your perfume and fragrances is kingdom business for the blessing of others for His glory.

Correlation of Fragrance and Age

"When I was a child, I talked like a child, I thought like a child, I reasoned like a child. When I became a man, I put the ways of childhood behind me." (1 Corinthians 13:11, NIV)

How old are you? I know there is an unwritten rule that we should not ask a woman's age, but how old are you, spiritually? By default, some fragrances are too mature for the younger woman, whereas other fragrances are not suitable for the mature older woman. Are you wearing the right fragrance given your age? Is it effective? Let's say you are a woman age forty-two. Do you still handle conflict and problems the same way you did as a seventeen-year- old girl? Do you require a daily milk bottle feeding of the Word or have you grown enough to satisfactorily digest the meat, the Lamb of God?

You can usually tell how old a woman is by the fragrance she wears. It's rare to find an older woman fragranced with cotton candy or a young woman smelling like an oriental musk. Yes, you have a choice in what scent you choose to wear, but every fragrance is not for everybody. We all develop at different paces. Have you ever observed a physically grown woman with adolescent behavior? It is not a pleasant sight. The same is true of the spiritual. Observing a spiritually grown woman who's been saved since the early 1800s, figuratively speaking, with the mindset of a child is disturbing. There are suitable and more appropriate fragrances for every age. As the result of extraction, there are three types of women when it comes to perfume. Transitioning in or out, we fit into categories of concrete, absolute, or an essential oil from the garden of Gethsemane. In the order preceded, the difference is the concentration of oil within.

Concretes

Concretes are affectionately known as the babes in Christ: fresh out of the womb born-again believers not yet skilled in righteousness. (Hebrews 5:13) They have a new relationship with Jesus and an innocent outlook on spiritual matters, oblivious to discerning false prophets or religious manmade rules of law. They have to learn what they can and cannot put in their mouths. Concretes also have an expected heavy dependency on older brothers and sisters in Christ to pacify them and initially teach them from the Word of God how to fight principalities and powers. Babes in Christ usually don't know how to pray for themselves and often get caught up in the titles of who's laying on of hands. With joy being full, their mustard seeds of faith have begun to grow as they learn how to walk by faith and not by sight, drinking the milk of the Word for nourishment of their spirit being and transformation of mind, forgetting the things of old as all has become new while pressing toward the mark for the prize of the high calling in Christ Jesus.

Absolutes

Absolutes derive from concretes after they mature into the spiritual adult. Pliny, a Roman naturalist, once said, "Young plants also have less perfume than old ones; the strongest perfume however of all plants is given out in middle age."

Absolutes have come into the knowledge of Christ, rightly dividing the word of truth. They can smell the enemy a mile away and know how to diffuse their fragrance and perfume to trample over serpents and scorpions, cancelling any plans or attacks of the enemy. (Luke 10:19) Absolutes are at the peak of their strength, feeding their spiritual beings the meat and the milk of the Word while also flowing in the principles likened to obedience over sacrifice. Due to the word saturated in their hearts over time, absolutes know how to call those things that are not as though they were, strategically decreeing and declaring the power of God as proactive, rather than reactive. However, absolutes--being mature--if not watchful can give way to temptations (Mark 14:38) toward complacency in their walk with Christ. After having been matured in the word, ignorance is no longer an excuse for a pass, although some may see "lukewarm" as a feasible option. 2 Peter 2: 20-22, NIV reads: "If they have escaped the corruption of the world by knowing our Lord and Savior Jesus Christ and are again entangled in it and overcome, they are worse off at the end than they were at the beginning. It would have been better for them not to have the way of righteousness, than to have known it and then turn their backs on the sacred command that was passed on them. Of them, the proverbs are true: A dog returns to its vomit."

Thus, the weight of responsibility for carrying the gospel, dying to self, and setting the example of servitude for others becomes greater.

Hebrews 5:12-14, NKJV reads:

12: For though by this time you ought to be teachers, you need someone to teach you again the first principles of the oracles of God; and you have come to need milk and not solid food.

13: For everyone who partakes only of milk is unskilled in the word of righteousness, for he is a babe.

14: But solid food belongs to those who are of full age, that is, those who by reason of use have their senses exercised to discern both good and evil.

Notice in verse 14 it says, "...their senses exercised to discern both good and evil." We have five senses, including the sense of smell. Notice that "senses" in verse 14 is used in the plural form, to give significance to more than one sense. The Bible does not state that one particular sense over the other is more important. Our sense of smell as we get older gives us the capability to discern both sweet-smelling and sour odors in the spirit realm.

In saying that, there is no excuse for foolishness just because it's a different face, but same situation. Absolutes have grown and learned to go around the mountain one time and keep it moving. Hebrews 6: 4-6 states:

4: For it is impossible for those who were once enlightened, and have tasted the heavenly gift, and have become partakers of the Holy Spirit,

5: and have tasted the good word of God... to crucify our Lord all over again.

Absolutes have grown into the wisdom within their walk in Christ, so that the relationship is not to be compromised for anything or anyone. They didn't walk this far by faith to go back to mess.

Essential Oils

Essential oils are the indispensable lifeline for absolutes and concretes. Essential, in this context, does not mean "vital." It means the inherent essence of a woman, the pure refinement and full development you can get only through aged experience and wisdom in the Lord. Ladies, we all have essential oils within us. However, this particular essence is not revealed until we have been fully matured. In Titus 2:3-5, the Bible states: "the older women likewise, that they be reverent in behavior, not slanderers (gossipers), not given to much wine, teachers of good things—that they admonish the young women to love their husbands, to love their children, to be discreet, chaste, homemakers, good, obedient to their own husbands, that the word of God may not be blasphemed."

A woman named Naomi in the book of Ruth, and King Lemuel's mom--also known as Solomon's momma--are exemplary models of essential oils. Naomi, in spite of her widowhood, losing both of her sons and her husband, was able to bless her daughter-in-law Ruth with great wisdom because of her oil (See Book of Ruth).

We all know about the Proverbs 31 woman, but let us perform a little background check on her. Did you know this woman bore a child out of wedlock with a very prominent and wealthy man via a one-night stand--all while her husband was away on government business? Oh yes, the highly esteemed Virtuous Woman had a rather unpleasant and dramatic past (like most of us who will honestly admit it) but she gives such wisdom about how to be a successful and pro-ductive loving wife, mother, and entrepreneur...the goals that we all strive to achieve in some manner. One cannot be a Virtuous Woman without having gone through learning or experience to back it up. Have you figured out her name yet? It is Mrs. Bathsheba, once wife of Uriah, later married to King David.

Essential oils carry great potency. There are some glories that we will not experience until we have walked with the Father for a long time. Have you ever just sat down in the presence or tutelage of an elder and listened to the wealth of wisdom they naturally pour out? I find it absolutely refreshing. Essential oils do not give way to worry or fear, because they have been there and done that, having seen the beauty and promises of the Lord fulfilled. God tells us in Isaiah 46:4, "Even to your old age, I am He. And even to gray hairs I will carry you! I have made and I will bear; even I will carry, and will deliver you." Don't let the slow walk and silver hair fool you. Grandma and the other elders know a thing or two about dropping it like it was hot and how to bounce back from spiritual setbacks.

James 1:11, NIV says "For the sun rises with scorching heat and withers the plant; its blossom falls and its beauty is destroyed." Long after their petals are crushed and pressed, the flower itself is no more --after they are gone, the essence of that plant will remain. It will either become compost to help nurture the soil for other flowers to grow, or live as the essence of oil in our lives. As it is written in 1 Timothy 5:17, "Let the elders who rule well be counted worthy of double honor, especially those who labor in the word and doctrine." Why is it that your great-aunt or grandmother's words stick to you like honey, sweetly lingering in your life from time to time? You honored her by listening to her, be it consciously or subconsciously, and she left you with her oil. She may no longer be with you, but the essence of her perfume will always remain.

Reflection: Developing in any of the stages as a concrete, absolute, or essential oil in Philippians 1:27, NIV Paul tells us that "whatever happens, conduct yourself in a manner worthy of the gospel of Christ."

Preservation

"He has preserved our lives and kept our feet from slipping."
(Psalm 66:9)

Ladies, we are all too familiar with the art of preservation. We use silk scarves, satin bonnets, bobby pins, rollers, and even wigs to maintain a hairstyle or hair objective in order to keep it fresh. I think the all-time favorite of our preservation routine is "sleeping pretty." God, as our Perfumer, uses the same concept for our lives. When God designs your signature fragrance, it is imperative for you to have a cover for preservation purposes. Without your cover, you become vulnerable to oxidation, premature evaporation, and contamination by outside influences that could possibly taint or ruin your fragrance. Being covered prevents degradation and exposure, and is a form of protection and care. We freeze vegetables and fruits to preserve them for later consumption. We wash clothes in cold water or dry clean them for longer wear life. Parents preserve their children, keeping them from hurt, harm, and danger, both seen and unseen, wherever possible. And just as parents do, the God we serve promised in 2 Timothy 4:18: "The Lord shall deliver me from every evil work and will preserve me unto His heavenly kingdom."

Preservation can take many forms and as a Perfumed Letter, we are preserved with oil. The anointing oil of Christ is a spiritual preservative that prevents rust, decay, and spoilage. Have you ever seen a woman in the house of the Lord, molding under an old anointing because God isn't moving like that anymore? In any case, the power of Christ can not only redeem and restore you; it will act as a preservative to keep you from stumbling. When we allow Christ to become our Lord, we are invigorated by His scent. We know the aroma of His presence as He enters a room. Our spiritual senses are awakened and our lives are forever changed. As we grow in Christ, developing a more intimate relationship with Him as our Lover, His oil begins to saturate us, rubbing off on us more with every encounter and embrace. I know when He holds me in comfort or in the moment of a blessing, the oil smells so good I have one of those "exhale" moments because He's so good to me.

After the butterflies and the honeymoon, we find ourselves fixed in complacency of servitude later on. Go to church on Sunday, check. I shouted and spoke in tongues. Sang in the choir, and served on hospitality team. We can get tired of the routine and covering, asking God and even screaming possible expletives from time to time. "Let me out! I'm ready! I thought about it, but, I didn't curse her out! My biological clock is ticking!" To be preserved doesn't always feel so good, because it is not set around our time schedule. Depending on the intended use of your perfume, you can be preserved anywhere from short periods of a few days to longer shelf life periods of months or years. While being preserved "for such a time as this," adjusting to patience when your nerves are already thin can be extremely frustrating. It could be any number of things: waiting on check, a degree, a child, buying a house, custody, getting out of debt, or even waiting for a husband. Yes, girlfriend, I'm there with you. I understand completely. The waiting game is not my cup of tea. I find myself wanting to "do a David" and ask God for forgiveness later, but I am yet learning my perfume and all that will come with it, while believing and trusting that God's timing is what's best. Do you want something good, or do you want God's best?

God is our covering. It is His responsibility to ensure that special storage and handling procedures are in place on your behalf...forever. (Psalm 121:8) The blood of Jesus covers all of our transgressions and rebellions—past, present, and future. The Bible says He died once and for all. (Romans 6:10) Whatever you did yesterday, to what you've already done today, toward what you will do tomorrow, Jesus has it covered. He gives you grace. His mercies are new every morning. Growing up in church, I've heard of parents giving their kids a pre-whuppin just in case they act up. Well, Jesus does the same thing; He ensures you have enough mercy to cover any wrongdoing, just in case. Honey, as a born-again Christian, you have a gift of repentance and no condemnation (Romans 8:1) from the Father, wrapped up in a goodie bag full of new mercies, but don't forget we forget we reap what we sow.

Natural and Spiritual Coverings

While you are here on Earth, God sends natural and spiritual coverings in the form of fixatives to preserve us in all facets of life. Fixatives are indispensable in helping us to develop into what God desires us to become. One fixative is that He commands his angels, concerning you, to guard you in all your ways; they will lift you up so that you will not strike your foot against a stone. (Psalm 91:11-12)

From the beginning, we are covered with parents or legal guardians who are mandated to train us in the way that we should go, so when we are old, (at the appointed time when our scent is released) we will not depart from it. We have other natural authority coverings or fixatives within teachers, employers, coaches, healthcare providers, policemen, and even the president of our nation. God in His infinite wisdom gives us spiritual coverings consisting of apostles, pastors, intercessors, and bishops to keep our preservation intact. Hebrews 13:17, NKJV says, "For He said in His word; to obey them that have rule over you for they watch and must give an account for your souls." Those people are strategically assigned in our lives. As the word of God reads further in Romans 13:1, NKJV: "Let every soul be subject to the governing authorities. For there is no authority except from God, and the authorities that exist are appointed by God. Verse 2: Therefore whoever resists the authority resists the ordinance of God, and those who resist will bring judgment on themselves."

Esther was a woman in the Bible who embraced both natural and spiritual coverings. We can find her story in The Book of Esther. She was orphaned, but raised in a God-fearing home under the care of her cousin Mordecai. Esther found favor in the sight of the king and because of her obedience toward God and her obedience to the natural covering of Mordecai, she saved her people from genocide.

If you don't submit to them, it will not be profitable for you. For example, God says we are to honor our parents, for if we do not, our lives will be shortened. God was not asking you to honor; He was telling you. He's only looking out for your benefit and His glory. Both the natural and spiritual coverings are there to protect you. It's very important that you submit to those who have been placed in your life as a covering. (Titus 3:1) Submission does not mean being a slave, but it means to be humble enough to allow someone responsibility for you and/or to press you out of pride and the like. Being attentive to your coverings is a preventive measure from the regrets of the shoulda, woulda, coulda and the infamous "Oh, if I had known then what I know now" cliché.

One manner of preservation is correction. Correction is a

preservative that will benefit you and bring glory to God. Do not twist your neck, roll your eyes, and mumble under your breath. Receive correction and move on. In Psalm 141:5, NIV it reads: "Let a righteous man strike me—it is a kindness; let him rebuke me—it is oil on my head. My head will not refuse it...." Sometimes we get caught up in tradition or the comfort of handling life a certain way, so much so that in order to receive that breakthrough, we need correction. Correction and obedience go hand in hand. They are not wants or maybes, but needs. We have a need for structure in our lives. For structure to be present, correction and obedience are warranted. We must be willing to accept them in order to "become," and fix our present state of being. Obedience breeds blessing. If you decide to abstain and disregard correction, you may end up bearing the consequences alone. (Proverbs 9:12)

Here's a hard truth: Proverbs 15:32 says that he who refuses correction is stupid. Ouch! The Bible isn't naming names now, but if the stiletto fits....

The Word of God tells us: "Do not despise or shrink from the chastening of the Lord or abhor His reproof." Real simple. Don't catch an attitude every time someone corrects you or tells you what to do in a manner that will benefit you. Grown people throw temper tantrums too. I know--I'm one of them. I don't know about you, but I'm one of the hard-headed kids in the kingdom. On more than one occasion, God had to call me by my first, middle, and last name, for me to KNOW I was in trouble. However, I know when God chastens us, it's a great example of His love. (Proverbs 3:12, Revelation 3:19) Good parents discipline their children. This may be a verbal scolding or getting a switch to that butt. Do you remember the day? I'm sure you can remember way back when you had to go pick your own. It was out of love, tough love. Correction isn't meant to be pleasant. It is not intended to just let you have your way. When you become a believer and you are His child, He expects you to act a certain way. He expects you to obey the rules and standards of His house. If you have an issue, get grown and get out. From correction, discipline, and instruction come knowledge and wisdom, which are both good for the soul.

When God corrects you, hope and pray that it is an immediate whuppin' so you can go ahead and get it over with. When He decides to correct you in the middle of the Christmas season, or two years after the fact, it can seem so cruel--but He's doing it because He loves you. Please know whenever the Holy Spirit gets your attention, His objective is to remove a chemical or danger that is stealing, killing, or has the potential to destroy your fragrance. It is never meant to condemn you. It's a loving way of telling you how to get back where you should be, in alignment with what you were created to do, and walk in who you were called to become. Don't get it confused--God is as loving as He is just, and He will allow certain conditions to come into your life. These conditions are a part of the composition to get you to fulfill your purpose. What you are going through, honey, isn't for you. You have a unique perfume that needs to be transpired through you for someone else.

There was a man in the Bible named Joseph who journeyed through the preservation process as well for the life of others, but not without pain. Disclaimer: Since we are speaking of a man, the outcome of his product was of course, cologne. We can find his story in Genesis Chapters 37, 39-45. Joseph was the baby of the family, Daddy's favorite, and the Bible says he was hated by his brothers. At a young age, God had given Joseph dreams of greatness and power. Excited, he described them to his family, but his father rebuked him and his brothers were jealous because these weren't just any dreams. Joseph's dreams represented that one day he would rule over them, and his family would bow down to him. As a result, Joseph's brothers were consumed with envy and conspired to kill him. One day they threw him into a pit which he could not get out of alone and sold him to traders, who in turn sold him as a slave into Egypt.

When we think of a slave, we imagine a person who is humiliated and beaten. While we may look immediately look at his situation and feel sorry for him, don't. God was still in control and He was working it out for Joseph's good. Amidst a bit of drama, God promoted him in the palace and he found favor in the eyes of Pharaoh. There came a famine upon the land and because of Joseph's promotion, he was in charge. His brothers came to the palace one day to ask for food, not knowing that Joseph was alive and now stood before them. Joseph immediately recognized who they were. He later revealed himself and told them "Do not therefore be grieved or angry with yourselves because you sold me here; for God sent me before you to preserve life...and God sent me before you to preserve a posterity for you in the earth, and to save your lives by a great deliverance." (Genesis 45:5 and 7, NKJV)

The aforementioned was just a short synopsis of a person who, just like you and I, had an oil, an anointing that needed to be pressed out for the sake of another. Who do you know, past or present, who was pressed to preserve you?

The Bible says that we go from glory to glory, meaning that God will *always* have something greater in store for us. Going from glory to glory requires us to go back to the Garden of Gethsemane. In Isaiah 48:10, it says: "Behold, I have refined you, but not as silver; I have tested you in the furnace of affliction." Merriam-Webster's dictionary defines refine as "to free from impurities." The tests and trials are there to help improve us, mature us, and educate us. The question we should be asking ourselves is: Do we put our own selves in this furnace of affliction? Either way, God is going to work it out for your good (Romans 8:28, NKJV), but I'm going to need us to stop blaming God for every crisis or challenge that happens in our lives. Let's be honest. God said He will not put more on us than we can bear, for He gives us grace to handle our business from day-to-day. He will make a way of escape (1 Corinthians 10:13, NKJV) when the situation warrants to preserve you.

Discretion will preserve you only when wisdom enters your heart, and knowledge is pleasant to your soul. Understanding will keep you. (Proverbs 2:10-11, NKJV)

Wisdom will preserve you. (Ecclesiastes 7:12)

Your own lips will preserve you. He who guards his mouth preserves his life.... (Proverbs 13:3, NKJV)

The Lord will preserve all who love Him....(Psalm 145: 20, NKJV)

Packaging

We cannot talk about preservation without speaking of the packaging. The preservation of perfume requires special handling and when stored properly, perfume can be long-lasting. The preferred manner of storing perfume is to keep it in its original packaging.

Adam and Eve had a lot to do with changing our packages. Tell me something. Who were you before the foundation of the world? God says He knew you way back when. To know someone is to have a personal relationship with them. It is more than a hi and bye passing on the street or a social media association. Do you remember Him when you were naked and unashamed? When Jesus was crucified, buried, and resurrected, He restored you to your original package. By His shed blood, He redeemed us from the law of hiding behind fig leaves to embracing our nakedness without shame. Original packaging comes in the form of redemption, according to the Word of God.

Prior to allowing Jesus to come into our lives, we were in sin. We were flaunting around beautifully, lost and godless, with lip gloss on and attitude ready. Our mindset was focused on doing our own thing. Then something amazing happened. The Holy Spirit intentionally brushed past us, catching our eye, and Jesus, being the epitome of a distinguished gentleman, walked up to our heart, knocked on the door, and introduced Himself. He didn't blow the horn from the driveway or say "Hey, girl! Shawty, you nice in that dress," He didn't ask what our sign was or whether we had kids; nor did He inquire about our cellular number; or even compliment how pretty our pedicure looked. He didn't ask if we had a man, for He knew He would be our everything. No games were necessary. He went directly to our hearts.

Yes, if you were like me, raised in church, can quote scripture, dress the part, and even speak in tongues on cue, but could be nominated for Best Backslider. However, none of it mattered because I didn't have a personal relationship with the Lord. The outside packaging didn't match the inside gift. Jesus was not my number one. I was--or whoever I happened to be with at the time filled that spot. For the longest time, I had one of those on again, off again relationships with Jesus. Honestly, He was a booty call some nights. I'd call Him in the middle of the night when I was worried or needed something, not because I loved Him and just wanted to be with Him.

Although not outwardly displayed, perfume has an expiration date. When the original packaging is changed with our consent (God gives us a choice) allowing sin to entertain us by decomposing the scent, our perfume's intended lifespan is shortened. Of course grace and mercy will follow us forever, but the receipt of eternal life after we have given our lives to the Lord is anointing given to us for a specified time and place. When we choose to be indolent and cease stirring up the gift God has given us, or nonchalantly use the power invested in us, the package is exposed to tampering.

Fine Print

Have you ever noticed that on perfume bottles or their packages, the ingredients are not listed? Don't take my word for it. Go look on your bathroom counter, dresser, or the vanity--wherever you keep your perfume and other fragrances. Take a good look and you will be surprised to find that the ingredients are not displayed. There is no indication by looking at the box packaging, or the bottle alone, the details of what make that scent pop. Why? Ingredients are not disclosed because they are considered trade secrets and patents. No one needs to know the "secret" formula used to produce your favorite perfume. How does it maintain the longevity of scent? It's all in the ingredients. For our sake, those ingredients may seem like hopeless and hellish situations or those long "in-between-waiting-on-God" experiences, but they are exponentially powerful in our development and deliverance, and His majestic glory. Anointing is not a one size fits all--many are called, but few are chosen. No one needs to know the absolute formula used to create that perfume. The ingredients are nobody's business. However, by default, after giving our lives to Christ, becoming Perfumed Letters, we are written testimonies that God and His word are real. We are certified living witnesses of what God can do. You may indeed be the only one presented to another who needs to see the transparency packaging of Christ written in your life before they decide to make a choice.

Brand Names

The Bible says the only thing better than perfume is your name, implying one's character. (Ecclesiastes 7:1, Proverbs 22:1) Think of every natural brand-name perfume on the market today. Each name carries with it a certain amount of clout that the consumer expects just by looking at the packaging. Don't allow and succumb to those naysayers categorizing you as a holy roller, religious fanatic or freak, or some might even say hypocrite (but remember your righteousness is a fact, not a feeling or an opinion) and that you need to get your life together. The devil is a liar who comes to steal, kill, and destroy. You got your life together the day you asked Jesus to come into your heart. The swag in your character has much bearing on your perfume. If you don't know who you are, you will never know your name or your worth. What good is having an anointing if the character does not match? The crazy thing is, even Satan knows who you are. The instant you discover who you really are, you are a serious threat to his kingdom because you have taken back reign over yours. Take off the heels and makeup. Pull back your hair in a ponytail, lace up the sneakers, and put a bit of Vaseline on your face. Fight back! Seek the Lord while He may be found to rock that brand name on purpose for kingdom business. If what you can do is the old windwheel, that's cool because you will mount upon wings as an eagle and whup Satan's tail. I mean when character is beckoned, you pick up a heavy-duty lock in the Word, like "No weapon for against me shall prosper" or "No grave trouble shall overtake the righteous" and bash the enemy's head in. If you know who you are, you won't cry victim, but victor! No need to be shy, for the kingdom of heaven suffers violence, but the violent take it by force. (Matthew 11:12)

Reflection: Preservation is much like God's chastening; it is a reflection of His love for you. Think of your natural and spiritual coverings, past and present. Which one has stood out the most? Why? If you didn't understand then, do you understand now, the truth of "how and why" God used them in your life to preserve you?

Single Mom's Preservation

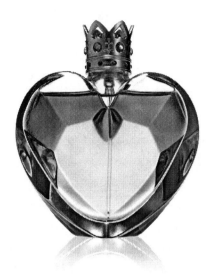

I know first-hand that being a single mother can be a difficult and challenging experience, but God has not forsaken you. It is of no consequence how you became a single mother: by choice, through adultery, playing house with the mindset that his sex game is so on point—you wanted to have his baby, the one percent affected on the pill, a bitter divorce, or rape. God will turn a bad situation into a blessed one in spite of the details. A woman in the Bible named Hagar was in such a situation. You can find her story in Genesis 21: 8-21.

Miss Hagar

Hagar was the maid of a couple named Abraham and Sarah. Sarah decided she did not want to wait on God's promise that He would bless her womb, and told Hagar to sex Abraham so that Sarah could have a kid. She wanted Hagar to be the surrogate. I'm sure Abraham didn't put up a fight. I mean really, what man would say no to a one-day pass? What kind of woman would give her man a pass in the first place? Sarah may have been a beautiful woman, to include her looks, but that day, she had a dumb asteroid moment. Hagar later ended up pregnant and gave birth to a son, Ishmael. Drama ensued shortly thereafter. Sarah regretted her decision and quickly dismissed Hagar, and told her and her son Ishmael to get the hell up out of her house. Yes, that was so grimy--and to add insult to injury, the man of house, Abraham, not standing up for his kid, sent them away with food and water into the wilderness.

This woman had nothing. Hagar had no job, no shelter, and no girlfriends to console her, nowhere to go. The weather was hot and humid. She couldn't call Abraham from the field and ask if he would take Ishmael for the weekend to spend some quality time with his son. It was just her and her baby, alone. This alone time became the best time for her and God to have a conversation.

Once the food and water were consumed, she laid her son down for a nap. Watching him sleep, she sat down across from Ishmael and reflected on the reality of what she had done. No woman in her righteous mind says, "I want to sleep with a man, get knocked up, and become a single mother." I don't recall any little girl growing up with those intentions. How could she say no? Sarah was her boss, her meal ticket. Sarah took her in and was like a mom to her. How could she just do her so dirty? She had been there for the both of them and now that she needed them, they were nowhere to be found. This was not what Hagar dreamed for the life of her child, especially to be without his father. She couldn't teach him to be a man. "Oh God," she muttered in tears, "What have I done?"

She sat watching him sleep soundly, but in regret, she stated sorrowfully in verse 16: "Let me not see the death of the boy." To paraphrase what she said to the Lord: *I don't want to live to see my child suffer because of my lack of judgment. I don't want to see his hurt and shame being raised without a father or a picture perfect family. I don't want to witness how he treats women because of how his father treated me. I don't want to see the generational curse I co-signed on because I spread my legs.* "She began to cry and cry aloud, crying herself to sleep." This would be the first of many times she would do this.

But get this. In verse 17, the Bible says that God heard the voice of the child. I had an epiphany because although Hagar cried out to God in those liquid prayers, God heard her, but He listened to her child. I don't care what you have done or the manner in which it was carried out, children have a special place in God's heart. In Psalm 127, the word of God states that children are a heritage of the Lord and the fruit of the womb is His reward. We love our babies, but be reminded that they are in our care for only a little while, for they are His reward. God will get the glory from your baby.

God gave Hagar the grace needed to be a single mother. In turn, He blessed her son Ishmael. God was with him growing up, and turned him into a great nation. (Genesis 21:18, 20)

Single mother, beautiful and strong you are. The wilderness you will experience is not the end of your life. I know you have grown exhausted from being so strong 24/7 and are feeling weak, with a small desire to just put your feet up and relax, if only for thirty seconds. I know how you feel. Trust and believe that Jesus is covering you with every step you take, preserving you, and He will give you rest. He will send you the help and grace you need. (2 Corinthians 12:9) Know that your preservation is not in vain. The pressure you feel right now is pressing out the oil for your perfume. It is a process of something in your oil that your child needs from only you, and like your breast milk, it's formulated especially for your baby. Yes, physically you may be without the other parent. But be encouraged, you are never alone. In John 14:17, Jesus said: "I will not leave you as orphans--comfortless, desolate, deprived, and helpless; I will come back to you." Don't worry about your child. God will be a Father to your child, covering him, for He has spoken in Isaiah 54:13: "Your children will be taught by the Lord."

A Bit of My Story

I have borne the pain of being a single mother and I am going through it at this very moment. A typical day: wake at 4:30 a.m. to spend some QT with the Lord; wake my son at 5:30 a.m. to get ready for school, fix breakfast (and I'm talking pancakes, bacon, eggs, and sliced fruit); drop him off to before care at the youth center and be at work sitting at my desk by 7:00 a.m. I work for the government, and the job and position in which I am currently placed is brutally demanding, from 7 a.m. to 4 p.m. given if overtime is not mandated. From there, I pick up my kid from after care and drive immediately to his professional tutoring session, which begins at 5 p.m. Stay with me now; the day is halfway over. After tutoring, I make the drive to the Scout meeting (which started at 6:00) and from there we drive home, eat dinner, and do homework. If all goes according to plan, he has his bath, bedtime story, prayer, and in bed by 8:30 p.m. When my son is in bed, then I begin on a few chores, my college coursework-- readings and research papers for school, and most days, I'm in bed by 12:30 a.m. That doesn't include attending Bible study, weekday errands, or his sports activities…take that to the max if I'm sick or have those serve cramps. Whoa! I know. I'm not the only single mommy pushing hard. We can't stop when we are sick, cramping, or just need a nap. It is by God's strength and His grace alone, sufficient for us every day, that we are able to do it all again the next day.

God Will Provide

An example of God's provision for the single mother can be found in 1 Kings 17. I have had pleasant and rewarding days, while others the pain some days is overwhelming and excruciating. I have cried enough tears to fill Lake Ontario over the past eight years. I know what it's like to wish the decision would rest on a partner's shoulders, or to want to go out to dinner or a family outing and silently hurt because the head of household does not exist to complete the picture.

I have been in a relationship where the man knew I was not the type of single mom unable to keep my feet and home and tend to my responsibilities, so he ended up milking me for my goodies, groceries, and grace. Oh, and the on-the-job-training he was a recipient of that would benefit the next one too. Girl, I know exactly what you are going through…and God does too.

I remember the first time I took my son on an airline flight. I was traveling to see my mother. He was about two months old. I was by myself, traveling with the two-in-one car seat and stroller, the baby bag, and my own carry-on. When it was time to go through security, I was getting ready to unload everything, take off my coat and shoes and his, make sure to separate the electronics in a separate box, break down the car seat and stroller, and hold my son at the same time. It was all the hassle of going through the security gate, but with an infant in hand as I didn't have that "extra pair of hands." Hundreds of people passed by and no one offered to help. God saw my need and covered me. He touched the heart of a pilot walking by who told me to hold the baby and he would break down everything and load it on the other side. Hallelujah!

My son is currently in Cub Scouts, and with the majority of activities in which they are involved in like BB gun shooting, carving, repairing, camping, et cetera; I would silently cry out to God about my son not having a father figure in his life to help him with this or that or be present to show support. I would cast my cares on the Lord, telling Him, as if He didn't already know, how hurt I was and how much I needed relief, or simply expressing myself, reminding God that I can't make his father fulfill his responsibilities and be a father to my son. God, I can't do this anymore, I'm tired!

Every year, the Scouts take part in an event called the Pinewood Derby. The rules are that each scout has to build his own car from scratch using a small block of wood, four wheels, and four nails. The design, color, and style are up to the participant. Now, I don't know the first thing about carving or shaving, and I do not own a drill. When the announcement was made the event was coming up and the details involved, I said aloud, "I don't know how to make a car." This was one of those silent "Help!" moments between me and God. The physical presence of a man to do this was absent. I needed the Lord's help. God indeed moved on our behalf. One of the den leaders sent me an e-mail and put me in contact with another Scout leader who was able to help. We met at his house and he kindly helped to carve, sand, and drill holes for the weights—donating his time to help my son make a car. Two days later, after we painted the car at home, he also aided in installing the axles and wheels and taking it on a test drive. I watched as he instructed my son how to hold the hammer and what pressure to use—guy stuff, you know? It may seem insignificant and trivial to some, but to a single mother without the knowledge or a partner to help, it can be devastating. Yes, Satan threw it up in my face: "You know his father should be here, what kind of mother are you, and this is your fault, this is the bed you slept in…" right in the middle of my blessing! Ugh! I dismissed his voice with the word that God supplies all of my needs. While holding back tears, I began thanking the Lord for answering my prayer. I was deeply grateful to the man whom I knew was God-sent. I know He hears the prayers of the righteous and He will deliver them out of ALL their troubles! (Psalm 34:17) Single mothers are not excluded from being preserved by the hand of God!

My child's father is not what I would call active in his life. I actively receive state- mandated child support on his behalf. When I describe active, I mean spending a weekend out of his "busy" schedule to pick him up, calling to checking on him regularly, affirming his love to our son and his belief in him on a consistent basis--not only on holidays or when he conveniently has a moment. Having done all to stand, I stand. I do my best to text and call my son's father, and involve him. I take the initiative to tell him the wonderful things our son is doing in school, grades, and other achievements because he doesn't care enough to call our son on his own. I do it as a courtesy. I cannot make him be there. I see on a regular basis the heavy heart of an eight-year-old, and eyes streaming with tears: "I wish my dad was here, I want to see my dad, is he coming?" It hurts to the core because despite all the Superwoman powers I possess, the thing he needs the most, I cannot provide. I am unable to give him or teach him in some ways what only a man can. I cannot fill the void in his heart for his father, but I know who can, and His name is Jesus. Ladies, if you are a single mom, doing it on your own, God knows and you are not alone. You cannot change your child's father; only God alone can do that. All power is in His hands. Here's what you can do. First, sincerely pray for your child's father that God will change his heart not to boast about being a baby daddy, but walk in the responsibility and honor of being your child's father. Secondly, continue to be a great mother, training your child up in the way that he should go and God will do the rest.

Jesus is my help! Satan likes to bring up old stuff, but you know what? There is therefore no condemnation for those who are in Christ Jesus. (Romans 8:1) I believe God has forgiven me. The difficult part was forgiving myself. I want you to understand, single mother, God has forgiven you too. He has seen the tears you wet your pillow with at night. He's working in your favor right now. I have seen the preservation covering of God in our lives, providing and protecting. Those times when I needed a male presence to do this or that, God blessed, and the need was fulfilled. What He has done for me, be encouraged that He will do it for you too.

If you are not a single mother, do not place yourself on a pedestal and belittle another. Sit down and hush. You may or may not know the gravity of the situation, and if you keep running your mouth and can't keep your attitude in check, beware that God has something for you too. "Touch not my anointed, neither do my prophets any harm...." (Psalm 105:15) Just saying, and I'm speaking to the "utmost, sanctified, saved since 1812, never dropped it like it was hot publicly or privately" women of God. If you happen to see a single mother in the grocery store parking lot unloading a ton of groceries or going through airport security, or you know her personally, offer to help. Believe me, even Superwoman greatly appreciates an act of kindness.

Reflection: You can look back at what happened and cry if you need to, but don't stay there. Love yourself by forgiving yourself, trust God to preserve you, and rest. Your preservation is not in vain. Every time you cry liquid prayers, you remind him of His promises for you. Be encouraged, my sister. From me to you, here's my favorite verse of scripture found in Psalm 62, 5-7 NKJV:

My soul wait silently for God alone,
For my expectation is from Him.
He only is my rock and my salvation;
He is my defense;
I shall not be moved.
In God is my salvation and my glory;
The rock of my strength,
And my refuge, is in God.

Wisdom of Application

"Wisdom is the principal thing; therefore get wisdom. And in all your getting, get understanding." (Proverbs 4:7)

In the words of CoCo Chanel, "A woman should wear perfume wherever she wants to be kissed." As daughters of the Most High, we should wear perfume wherever simply because it is the wisdom our reasonable service. (Romans 12:1) As wisdom is beyond skin deep, it penetrates the pores in the same manner perfume does. How must we go about applying it?

The first objective in learning to apply perfume is that everything must be done decently and in order. (1 Corinthians 14:40) Therefore, one must realize there are right and wrong ways of application. We can decide to apply perfume in ignorance and stupidity for something other than God's glory. For example, picture a beautiful woman like you taking a spa bath at the local sewer treatment plant. That's absolutely ridiculous, right? Well, applying stupidity would be putting perfume on a dirty body to cover a foul odor. Putting perfume on a dirty body is just unacceptable. That is not ladylike, it's nasty. It's like spraying air freshener in the bathroom after you've done number two. I don't care if you use spring orchard scented spray, it will not eliminate the odor. The air freshener will only coat it. The atmosphere's smell will still be funky. It's just a lighter scent of stank. We do not want to put on perfume that way. The Word of God describes it best in Proverbs 11:22, NKJV: "As a ring of gold in a swine's snout, so is a lovely woman who lacks discretion." We have more class and dignity--right, ladies?

Begin by showering in righteousness (Isaiah 45:8) and using a 2-in-1 repentance body wash and scrub in the blood of Jesus. Have you ever been involved in a situation of dirty gossip, backstabbing, revenge, sleeping unequally yoked with the enemy, etc.? Have you ever just wanted to start over, and apologizing didn't cleanse the residue of guilt and shame? Please understand that Christ died once and for all. (Hebrews 9:28) He died one time for all of your past, present, and future sins. Yes, I said future sins. I'm being real. As long as we are rocking our oh-so-fabulous body silhouettes on this earth, we are going to slip up, whether it is done intentionally or by accident. The key is to repent and keep it moving. True repentance is not just saying you're sorry, or a real quick-fast, "Oh, Lord forgive me" (but in your mind, not really meaning it, because you KNOW you're going to do it again). True repentance is drifting 180 degrees.

You have to mature and progress to a point in your spiritual walk with Christ that being led away by your own desires and doing your own thing is silly because you don't want to grieve the Holy Spirit. While we are on that thought, I'm going to need you stop blaming God for everything this side of heaven and yet on the other hand crediting Satan for the things you have gotten your own self into. Honestly, when you get to a certain point, you know the enemy is as dumb as a box of rocks. You know he has no power and certainly no game. God gives you a choice. Satan gives you a suggestion. There is power in either, but only if you allow it. God tells us to choose life. There's life in repentance. When you get to that point of being stuck-up in pride and you're too good to admit you've messed up--well honey, you are giving an invitation for death to come in and make himself comfortable. So go ahead, get it over with and repent. It feels a lot better than getting a bikini wax. Here's a bonus: If you follow the directions for this body wash found in 1 John 1:9, you'll notice it has a bit of pampering—Jesus will cleanse you. You don't have to do it. Gotta love it!

When was the last time you allowed God to get into the shower with you? Oh, how intimate a treat it is for a couple to spend quality time in the shower, completely naked and vulnerable. I remember being in a relationship with a former lover and desired the shower scene. Both of us were in the shower, but he washed himself and promptly got out. Needless to say, the moment vanished. He never sensed that I wanted something more. He was more concerned about the water bill or getting out and going to sleep. I'm shaking my head thinking about it, but thank God for deliverance! I had an earnest desire for the impurities on me to be cleansed by his hands, but he chose not to care and failed to recognize my vulnerability "to become" to him more giving when cleansed and refreshed.

With God, I have discovered it is a daily retreat to let go and allow Him in to pamper me. God cares about our vulnerabilities and knows those intimate moments in the shower with Him are special, as it is to His glory to have a clean and ready vessel.

The deep-cleansing body wash and scrub are thorough, and powerful enough to go through to the inmost parts. (Hebrews 4:12) They will create in you a clean heart and you will be washed whiter than snow to get that sparkly-clean feeling. They will do wonders for your body and your heart, giving you a heart of flesh and not a cold-hearted one of stone.

In John 14:23 it is written: "If anyone loves me, he will keep my word; and my Father will love him; and we will make our home with Him." Referring to love, we know love is an action verb. If you love Christ, you'll want to be clean and stay clean with His word. This is why you should do at least a mini personal spa with the Lord on a daily basis and cleanse yourself before you put on a garment of praise or your robe of righteousness. I strongly emphasize the importance of getting so fresh and clean prior to rocking that perfume.

Another key point following in John 14:24 is "He who does not love me, does not keep my words; and the Word which you hear is not Mine, but the Father's Who sent me." When we are keeping the Word of God in our hearts, the fruit will show. It will be obvious in lifestyle, conversation, and our circle of friends. The word of God is more than a t-shirt, a cross on a necklace, or something entertaining to do on Sunday. It is the life. The Word, metaphorically speaking, is a body wash for His spirit to purify ours. When David said, "create in me a clean heart and renew a steadfast spirit within me," he was making reference to the Word of God cleansing his heart.

What happens if you want to "let the house go" for a while—and take a mini vacation from the temple? The Bible speaks of a man who went out of his house and returned, to find it clean, empty, swept, and in good order. However, being led away by his own desires, the unclean spirit he allowed to return, made his soul (mind, will, and emotions) worse than the last state. (Matthew 12:43-45) Jesus originally cleaned the house and kept it clean by the man daily renewing himself in the Word. How do we keep it clean? Read the Word.

Jesus is speaking in John 15:3, stating "You are already clean because of the Word which I have spoken to you." This is the reason it's vitally important for us to be both hearers and doers of the Word. A good soak in the Word not only cleanses you, but makes you smell good, too. And that scent is like honey to a bee, attracting others to the Christ in you. Continuing on to John 15:22 Jesus said: "If I had not come and spoken to them, they would have no sin, but now they have no excuse for their sin." As Jesus speaks the Word into your heart, it is hidden to keep you from sinning. Now as long as we are in this human experience, there is a possibility of us getting mucky, but there's no excuse to be dirty. You know what I'm saying? No excuses for "I didn't know." God said if we do get a little mud on ourselves, if we confess our sins, He is faithful and just to cleanse us from all unrighteousness. (1 John 1:9)

In Ezekiel 36: 25-27, 29, NKJV God said that He will not only cleanse you, He will deliver you from what made you dirty in the first place.

Psalm 19:12…God will cleanse you from secret faults.

In order for the perfume (anointing) to work, you must put it on. Where to apply? Your pulse points of course…your mind, will, and emotions. Secondly, realize that manifestation of the perfume works from the inside out. As mentioned earlier in the text, perfume once applied penetrates deeply, much like the Word of God in the inward parts into our pores beneath the surface. We must remember due to the strength of perfume transporting through our pores to the inside of our being, we have to be watchful of what comes out, positive or negative. (Matthew 15:10-11) To apply correctly for your individual lifestyle, please use as directed according to the word of God, in the following manner for best results.

Layering

The second objective we want to understand is to apply in layers. For the first layer, we want to lotion up with a renewed mind which has the active ingredients: wisdom scented with knowledge. We don't want to walk anywhere ashy in the anointing. A renewed mind is more of a heavy body crème or butter that locks in moisture of godly thinking and godly choices. This cannot happen if you do not renew your mind daily in the Word so that we can have the mind of Christ.

Recommendation: Ensure that you get wisdom and knowledge. To have one without the other is just ignorance, and ignorance can dry out your Word.

Have you ever showered with righteousness and awakened your spirit with the fragrances of Joy or Praise in the morning and by the time you drove on the parking lot to work, somehow your scent dried and you found yourself wearing the perfume "Not Today"? What happened? You forgot to apply that Mind Renewal lotion.

The same of the natural realm is first true of the spiritual realm: the drier your skin is, the less ability you will have to retain your fragrance. Women who have oilier skin tend to hold onto their fragrances longer. Women with oily skin tend to spend more time in the anointing (in Christ) attain more of a youthful, supple appearance, aging with grace versus the woman with dry skin being led away by her own desires, whose scent evaporates rather quickly, rapidly aging on account of sin.

When wisdom is applied as directed from the Perfumer, there is a 100% guarantee that you will receive promotion, honor, grace, and glory. (Proverbs 4:5-9, NKJV) The more you keep yourself moisturized in the oil (His anointing), the longer you will be able to retain your fragrance.

Reflection: Is your daily beauty regime similar to the word of God above? If not, what adjustments should you make in order to change? Are you allowing God to pamper you—showering you in His righteousness--or are you being showered independently by the world's standards, which are unfortunately creating a grimy residue building up on your heart?

How to Make Your Scent Last

"Let us throw off everything that hinders and the sin that so easily entangles...." (Hebrews 12:1)

Have you ever wondered why your perfume does not last? Part of our normal beauty regimen for each day's agenda is to spray a bit of smell-good on. Sadly, we realize a short time later the scent has gone and we are reapplying before lunch. One key piece of wisdom in the longevity of your scent is to lay aside every weight we easily get entangled in. There are many different factors to account for this weight, such as a woman's diet, kryptonite, immediate environment and secret stress level--all have the capability to alter or evaporate your scent.

The company you keep, be it negative or positive, is a major component of your scent lasting or quickly evaporating. Our girlfriends, even guy friends and long-time BFFs—saved, and especially those who are non-believers--may indeed have caring hearts and good intentions, but according to purpose of your perfume, they have the possibility to deteriorate your scent.

If we are not with Him to include those within our vicinity, then we are against Him. No love lost. God loves you no matter who you hang with. He loves you, not necessarily what you are doing. With some individuals, you may have to pray and love them from a distance. The book of Ecclesiastes 10:1, NKJV makes it clear: "Dead flies make the perfume's ointment give off a stench." How is this possible? The Bible says in 1 John 4:5-6; "They [referring to dead flies] are of the world, therefore they speak as of the world, and the world hears them. We are of God. He who knows God hears us; he who is not of God does not hear us. By this we know the spirit of truth and the spirit of error." In other words--honey, let them keep talking. Pray for them, for they know not what they do--and keep it moving. God will bless you with the right friends who will encourage you and not inhibit your relationship with God.

Kryptonite

Believer on non-believer, every woman has kryptonite--it's not just a member of the opposite sex. It could be ice cream, an immense desire for acceptance, a lust for money. The kryptonite isn't the problem. It's your reaction to it. Your kryptonite could be that cigarette, excessive sleep, tithing on occasion. Kryptonite is that thing that makes you weak in your knees where your heart has not set a boundary. For example, if you entertain his call or accept his invitation to dinner or a visit, because he is your kryptonite with the untrained flesh hollering, you're going to end up sexing him something serious or exerting a bunch of energy arguing, and in either case feel emptier than you did before. Own up to it; the soul tie is still there. Yes, you got saved--your flesh did not. The enemy knows this and will continue to play you until you get it right and resist and then keep resisting. (James 4:7) Believe me, I know it's hard

and your flesh is screaming--don't allow yourself in that situation...
anymore. Watch and pray. Resist and run.

Slip up? God is merciful and full of grace, and your righteousness will remain intact. Confess, and He is faithful and just to forgive
and cleanse from the unrighteousness. Move on. I hear you. Yes,
that's easier said than done--but lady, you have to walk in the Spirit.
(Galatians 5:16) If you don't, that spirit of kryptonite will continue
to plague you, souring your scents by placing an invisible wall between you and God. You will feel like God hates you or won't bless
you anymore, or you have to work for His love and forgiveness. It
will seem like you can't open your mouth to pray or lift your hands
to praise. The desires are strong and you don't know what you want
anymore. God, kryptonite, or both? It sounds crazy, but when we are
entangled with these various weights, we sometimes can't see straight
or walk upright, so the Bible tells us to walk in the Spirit (Galatians
5:16-17) and we won't get caught up creating a disconnect between
us and God. I know you may not feel like forgiving or being gentle
when someone may actually deserve to get slapped or put in place
with the power of not-so-nice words, but you are called to a higher
standard. By accepting a kryptonite's invitation, our scent loses its
power. Jesus died on the cross for this very reason: to remove the veil
(2 Corinthians 3:16) from the entanglements past, present and future.
Jesus loves you regardless. Kryptonite is not going away, but you can
keep your tolerance for it in check. Make your scent last by walking
in the Spirit.

Daughter of Christ, you have the power to trample over all the
feeble power of the enemy. As the word reads in 1 John 2:27, "The
anointing which you have received from Him abides in you...the
same anointing teaches you concerning all things, and is true and is
not a lie." You have already overcome the world because He who is
in you is greater. Walk in the Spirit and let Him be greater.

Friends, Family, and Other Folk

You know if you get to hanging around her or the girls again, it's going to be one big gossip session, full of meaningless he said-she said, dramatic woe-is-me conversation. Maybe you just gave your life to the Lord and your old circle of friends you grew up with or have other longtime friendships, now ridicule your lifestyle change by taunting you. At every chance that opens the opportunity, they revert back to remind you of the old you and what you all used to do. They persist in constantly reminding you, sarcastically, not to forget where you come from, because they know the "real" you. They smile and bless with their mouths in support and congratulations to you, but inwardly they curse every move you make. And oh, don't mess up in front of them. A Christian with a negative moment is the icing on the cake to some. They seem to know the Bible inside and out, judging you on what a "professing Christian" who knows the Lord should and should not do, while you know good and well they aren't trying to live for Christ AT ALL. Oooohhh, I know--that gets under my skin sometimes, but I have to pray, "Father, forgive them, because they have no clue to what they are talking about," and keep it moving. It's not them, it's the spirit they are being puppeted by .

Please evaluate your friendship circle. Despite their different personalities, to a certain degree all are a reflection of you. Could it also be that you have chosen a person placed into your life for a season giving them a position of lifetime status? As a child of God with a gift of discernment, God will let you know with great clarity when it's time to cut them off. You will sense friction and uneasiness, not in comparison with an argument, but you won't be able to shake the feeling that something just isn't right about this anymore. You will feel that tug in your spirit, of God taking your hand and telling you it's time to go. The environment is no longer comfortable. You can fake all day the need to keep this friendship, but it will continue to rip you apart. His thoughts and His ways are higher than ours. (Isaiah 55:8-9)

The longer you stay and try to hold on, the more you are going to feel trapped, and the harder it will be to let go. It does not matter if the friendship or relationship was for over a decade or however long; when God says no—enough is enough. The pressing and extraction will have you kicking and screaming, but know it's for your good. God will bless you with right, godly friendships and relationships to make your scent last. When I finally gave up a nearly decade-long friendship, because of the deepening relationship in my walk with Christ and the coming of age with my perfume, I counted the loss of the friendship a gain for Christ. Surprisingly, I was not sad about letting go, but more excited than ever to know that God was directing my paths, helping me to make my scent last.

Here's a heads up: Satan and his boys are going to come at you harder than before whenever you decide to choose life. When it's time to break off that friendship or relationship, every little thing will be magnified to keep your focus on it. Yes, those petals may hurt when they are removed and the agony of the press intensified, but you will be thanking God later on.

The walk of faith is challenging, but keep pressing forward. You may be trying to get out of debt, slowly getting delivered from depression and negativity, or on the patch to quit smoking. Maybe you have been clean from alcohol for several weeks now, or even decided to stop playing house with the boyfriend. Thank you, Jesus! Greater days are coming for you. Everyone isn't keen on accepting Christ, especially if you have matured and grown away from friends and family. Do not be discouraged. If whoever does not receive you nor hear your words, when you depart from that house or city, Jesus said to shake it off. (Matthew 10:14) People can say whatever whenever, but it's what God thinks of you that matters.

Fine Print

Proverbs 12:26, NKJV: "The righteous should choose his friends carefully, for the way of the wicked leads them astray." Seriously, if you are living for Christ, doing the best you can in Him, consistently hanging around what you know isn't good for you will eventually rub off and lead you away from Him.

Proverbs 14: 7, NKJV: "Go from the presence of a foolish man, when you do not perceive in him the lips of knowledge."

Proverbs 13:20, NKJV: "He who walks with wise men will be wise, but the companion of fools will be destroyed."

Perfume and fragrance can be wasted if released early, and both can go bad just sitting. Perfume has an expiration date. Time is in God, God is not in time. The Word says in the book of Ecclesiastes 3:11, "God made everything beautiful in its time." The anointing (your perfume) is set for a designated time and specified place while you are here in this earthly realm. Be cognizant of releasing too soon or too late. If the perfume is not as strong or as potent as it used to be, the contents within it have changed or shifted. What once was a sweet fragrance for a certain time will turn sour if not used within that hour—repelling your blessings, those resources, divine favors and interactions needed to fulfill your purpose at that time. Could it be you are at the right age and scent is not lasting because you are not pouring anything out, restoring in order to be filled? Make your scent last by allowing your cup to overflow in its time, and use your perfume to pour Him into others. As you do so, you may be the one to plant the seed, while another waters it, but God will make it grow. (1 Corinthians 3:6)

You Are What You Eat

What are you eating? Are you snacking on the devil's tantalizing desserts behind closed doors, out of the church's view? Are you eating the world's fad diets for quick sugar highs and temporary lifestyle improvements, or have you dined on the Bread of Life for daily strength? Jesus told us, "Man shall not live by bread alone, but by every word that proceeds from the mouth of God."(Matthew 4:4, NKJV) If you are not eating the Word, are you dining solely on the reality entertainment and gossip magazines that profit absolutely nothing? Instead of committing your works to the Lord, so that He will establish your thoughts and trusting that He will direct your paths, are you feeding on horoscopes and psychics to get an answer right away? Oh, and the fad diets of inconsistently sowing your seeds of tithes and offerings out of habit or going to church to mark it off on your good Samaritan list--stop it. Are we saved, for real?

Eat healthy and we will live healthier lives. The word of the Lord in Isaiah 55: 2-3 reads:

> "Why do you spend money for what is not bread and your wages for what does not satisfy? Listen carefully to Me, and eat what is good, and let your soul delight itself in abundance. Incline your ear and come to Me. Hear, and your soul shall live...."

You will stunt your growth if you do not eat daily. Growing up in Christ, it is okay for babies do certain things because it's considered cute. Babies (concretes) need help holding a bottle and a bib to wipe up slobber. Children need someone to give them a Band-Aid and then kiss it and make it better after a fall. When you grow up as an absolute and essential oil, you recognize that when you fall, you can get back up seven times if need be (Proverbs 24:16), laying hands on yourself and keep it moving. I am not telling you to forsake the power of two in agreement. Sometimes you do need to go in prayer with another believer. However, when you lose the need for a pacifier—you don't need to be in the prayer line asking for a milk bottle on the altar every Sunday because your heart doesn't want to receive the truth for deliverance and you don't want to stop doing what it is you are doing. Others are captivated by an audience and seek the attention of being seen. Have you not grown up enough in the word to know that you can put your hands on yourself and pray? Keep on trying to save your life and you are bound to lose it. If you aren't giving it to God, who are you giving it up to? You need to get back to Jesus being your number one. Remember when He meant everything to you? You wouldn't compromise your relationship with Him for anything. You talk to everybody else, but won't say good morning to Him or thank Him for a blessing you have received. As Reverend Marvin Sapp phrased it, don't be a "conditional praiser," giving God praise and thanks only when He blesses you or answers a prayer, yet after that you have nothing to say to Him until you are again in need. Grow up. Yes, Jesus is our salvation, but he is more than Captain Save 'Em. He's more than an AKM--Automatic Kingdom Money.

Stress...of Secret Sin

I don't mean the normal stresses of life; this context refers to the stress of secret sins. These secret sins are not the shortcomings your girlfriends know about or the ones you are trying to hide anonymously on Twitter. These are the sins that you will take to your grave. At every opportunity, somehow you allow Satan and his team to entice your flesh to indulge in its guilty pleasures. You have the Christian hug down, you are fluent in church phonetics and most definitely know how to smile and lift up your hands on cue, but this secret sin has engulfed your life, so it is a stress that burdens everything in your life. You have hidden it so well that your flesh doesn't bother warring with the spirit, because you have become it.

Luke: 8:17: "For nothing is secret that will not be revealed, nor anything hidden that will not be known and come to light."

Deep-Seated Disorder

There was a man in the Bible who was so stressed out because of a secret sin, it became known as a deep-seated disorder. (John 5:1-9, 14) Deep things have roots, and I believe it was one of those sins he may have struggled with before he gave his life to Christ. It probably originated during childhood or adolescence. Fast forward to adulthood—he was now sanctified and saved, yet he would pray seeking God for deliverance, get delivered, and slowly somehow he kept getting pulled back into "yesterday." His house, the temple of the Holy Spirit, would be clean and swept for a few months, and then he would go on vacation. He would leave it unattended, with his guard down, and as a consequence, come home and find it in a worse state than before, thus making the sin a secret, a disorder deep-seated and never fully dealt with.

As my momma has told me on many occasions, you have to be tired of being tired. It is true that change will not happen until you do, and this man had come to that point. He said, "Lord, I'm tired and I don't want to be here living with this anymore." Of course Jesus had heard it all before and asked him directly, "Do you want to be healed?" Seriously, do you want to be made whole?

Many Christians go to the altar with wrong motives, and when the laymen or the pastors are praying for you and with you, it's on an empty head and an empty heart. They actually like being sick and the attention attracted because of it. These Christians have this one phrase in common: "I'm waiting on the Lord; He knows my heart."

Please believe that God knows the secrets of the heart and the cause of your deep disorder that is privately kept from the view everyone else. Deep-seated disorders, these secret sins, can and will deter your perfume or fragrance's longevity.

Let's get on the grind right now. There are some in the body of Christ with a deep mental disorder called Munchausen syndrome. They are comfortable just "waiting on God." They do nothing at all, and have no initiative. They enjoy being the center of attention in the sense of gaining all sympathy. They are fake and exaggerate their condition. According to doctor Marc D. Feldman, a psychiatrist and author of Playing Sick?; Untangling the Web of Munchausen Syndrome, Munchausen by Proxy, Malingering, and Factitious Disorder:

"People with...Munchausen syndrome feign, exaggerate, or actually self-induce illnesses. Their aim? To assume the status of 'patient,' and thereby to win attention, nurturance, and lenience from professionals or nonprofessionals that they feel unable to obtain in any other way. Unlike individuals who engage in malingering, people with factitious disorder and Munchausen syndrome are not primarily seeking external gains...though they may receive them... In some cases, the fabrication or induction of illness is an expression of jealousy, rage, or the desire to control others. They deliberately mislead others into thinking they ... have serious medical or psychological problems, often resulting in... hospitalizations, and even surgery . . . that they know are not really needed. In short...Munchausen syndrome... involves illness deception, or "disease forgery." They may feign illness...falsify lab results...exaggerate a medical problem—e.g., by claiming occasional mild back pain is crippling... aggravate an existing ailment—e.g., by manipulating a wound so it doesn't heal... induce an actual illness—e.g., by injecting themselves...to cause a raging infection."

Dr. Feldman goes on to say, "...these people live within private hells of their own creation, unable to experience the fullness and joy of life." These people play victim well and use their scent to play on emotion. People who are gullible fall for this mess, but those of us who know truth rightly divide it. (2 Timothy 2:15)

Crippled Compassion

Personally, something I have struggled with is my mercy-compassion gift. I tend to have a mercy gift that is out of control. I believe in showing compassion and giving people the benefit of doubt. Life happens. God has shown me mercies I know I don't deserve--why not give the same courtesy to others?

In a previous relationship, the guy, whom I cared deeply for (and by the way, whom I was unequally yoked up with) desired a certain piece of equipment for his business that cost approximately four thousand dollars. What did I do? He couldn't afford his own stuff and because I had foolishly loved him, I entertained the spirit of my enemy, not thinking about Christ, doing all kinds of stupid stuff trying to get ahead of God. I showed compassion for him, took money out of savings, paid the bill in full, and had the equipment sent directly to his home a week or so before Christmas. I blindly looked at it as an investment because if I have the mentality that if I have it to bless you, I will not withhold it from you. He didn't treat me fairly, nor did he have the capacity to pour into me the love given to him, and I had stayed while having an on-again, off-again booty-call type relationship with Christ, accelerating the decomposition of my fragrance. I did not apply wisdom or treat myself to a mini spa in the Word. The enemy had access to an open door. The enemy knew who I was, and my fragrance of compassion was being poured out at the wrong time. My worth was milked, soured, and abused. I compromised my relationship with Christ and who I was in Him as a Perfumed Letter.

Thank God for deliverance! You know you have been delivered when those same people puppeted by the enemy call, text, or e-mail in a certain manner to get your vulnerability exploited again cause they think they know you to use you for their benefit, yet it no longer moves you to act on their behalf. The enemy hates it when you have that upper hand. Make your scent last by knowing who you are in Christ, like right now.

Immediate Environment

Do not despise your current trial and circumstance. God may be allowing that test to hide you. Scientifically speaking, it is recommended that perfumes are kept hidden in dark, cool places to prolong the longevity of aroma. Cool, dark places--sounds like…ahem…valleys, right? "Yea though I walk through the valley…." (Psalm 23:4)

Valleys aren't five-star resorts. It's a BYOB--Bring Your Own Bible-- and work-out-your-own-salvation type of place. It is good to be in the valley. (Psalm 119:71) If a perfume is exposed to humidity and constant heat, the contents will quickly deteriorate and evaporate. I know it can feel devastating that God put you in a particular position and place, but He's secretly hiding you to openly reward you, for His glory. Read the book of Jonah in its entirety—it's a short story of the Bible about a man named Jonah, which can offer a bit of experience and counsel in this area. You may not be where you want to be and believe me, I understand fully, but reflect on the tremendous progress of how far you've come as a way of making your scent last.

Psalm 19:12-13, NJKV: "Who can understand his errors? Cleanse me from secret faults. Keep back your servant also from presumptuous sin; Let them not have dominion over me. Then I shall be blameless, and I shall be innocent of great transgression."

Reflection: How can you make your scent last? Hebrews 12 tells us to lay aside every weight. How do you do that? Make a choice, but it's strongly suggested that you choose life. Walk in Spirit. You don't have to show yourself strong, but be strong in the Lord and in the power of His might. Let Jesus help you with your bags. Let him take out the trash. Lady, you know you haven't been getting the best beauty sleep because the foul odor of miscellaneous things has been keeping you awake. He told you to "take My yoke upon you and learn of Me…for I will give you rest for your souls." (Matthew 11:29, NKJV) What choices do you need to make today to make your scent last?

Signature Fragrances of Christ

"By this we know that we abide in Him and He in us...."
(1 John 4:13)

A signature is a distinctive marking on something which readily identifies something else. There are several fragrances that have Christ's signature, His seal of approval. The following list is not all-inclusive.

Worship

Worship is one of my favorite fragrances. It's the one-on-one intimacy of affectionately giving pure adoration to Him that I find invigorating; it's a time when I get to savor and bask in His presence. David tells us in Psalm 45:11, "Because He is your Lord, worship Him." Worship can be seen as an outward public display of affection for our Savior and Lord in church, but it's oh-so-very private. It is more than the lifting of hands, music, praise, and tears. All those are outward manifestations and expressions of how you feel when worshipping Him. Worship is an intimate internal expression of exaltation for the King.

Avid wearers of this fragrance do not come with hands out asking for a blessing or a need for something to be fixed. The women who wear this fragrance simply come with open hearts to indulge in pure intimacy with Lord for who He is, not for what He's done. Just spending quality time with Him is enough. Worship is presenting your body as a living sacrifice daily before the Lord. It is giving Him all of you—no holding back. It is inclusive of your heart, attitude, emotions, and behavior. This is worshipping in spirit and truth. Worship is being unashamed of your nakedness before Him, for you know He isn't concerned with your vivacious curves, or your stretch marks, because fearfully and wonderfully made are you. (Psalm 139:14) When a woman fragrances herself with worship, she is one with the spirit and comes into the truth: Jesus is much more than Savior; but He is Lord of her life, and therefore worship becomes a lifestyle.

When you worship Him, you are telling Him how much you love Him. It is not something cute to do on Sunday so you can get a gold star of man-made recognition. Worship is adoration so deep that it is immeasurable. You would do anything to be in His presence and seek Him with all your heart, soul, and mind. You make time to spend some quality time to seek His face and be in His presence. Fragrancing yourself with worship, you can understand intimacy one has with Him. David puts it this way in Psalm 63:1-4:

"O God, You are my God; early will I seek You; my soul thirsts for You in a dry and thirsty land where there is no water. So I have looked for You in the sanctuary, to see Your power and Your glory."

Psalm 62: 5-7: "My soul waits silently for God alone. For my expectation is from Him. He only is my rock and my salvation; He is my defense; I shall not be moved. In God is my salvation and my glory; the rock of my strength, and my refuge is in God."

Psalm 84: 2: "My soul longs, yes even faints for the courts of the Lord; my heart and my flesh cry out for the living God."

When would be the best time to wear this? Well, anytime is a good time to worship the Lord. When something happens like the death of a relationship, or someone dies or is separated from your life, it's a perfect time to put on worship. (2 Samuel 12:16-20)

Scent of Brokenness

The worst place to be is often the best place to be according to God. It's not that God wants us to be literally broken, but if you are honest with yourself, sometimes you need to be broken. We need to take off the tough-girl mask and the Superwoman cape and let Him know we can't do this alone. Tell him you refuse to. I know I do. I have had many conversations with the Lord. Jesus is the one individual you can trust without holding back. You can trust Him with your heart and your deepest desires. No matter how dark the secret is and how insignificant you think your idea is, it's okay to be vulnerable with Him. Don't cover yourself with fig leaves; you know they're itchy and bothersome, like panties that ride up, so don't be afraid to be you or be broken. It's okay to be naked before Him. When He looks at you and sees the brokenness, He's looking at a reflection of himself. They that worship Him, must worship Him in spirit and in truth. Psalm 51:17, NJKV says: "The sacrifices of God are a broken spirit, a broken and contrite heart." This does not mean broken as in broken- down, pitiful, and misery has moved in as your roommate. Women of the faith are the strongest and toughest women I know, but hold great fragilities inside themselves. Our greatest weakness is our greatest strength. (2 Corinthians 2:10) When you let go of the attitude of "I can do this myself and I got it, and I can open my own door…" within that pride and ego your tenderness is revealed. Wearing the Scent of Brokenness, you may feel like a sucker and carry a disappointment so deep it leaves a scar, because the one you love--partner, family, or friend--takes advantage of you. That's okay. When you are vulnerable and broken, that's when you are available to hear Him with clarity and you make room for Him to fix it, working it out for your good. (Romans 8:28)

When you are alone, that's when He seems to show up and hold you the longest. You know how men seem to be more willing to approach a woman who is alone rather than a woman in the midst of a crowd of girlfriends (distractions)? Jesus doesn't go anywhere He's not invited. However, you are more approachable and willing to listen when you don't have so much going on. It is in this vulnerable scent of brokenness that we find Him holding us closer than ever. We can't fix everything. We weren't made to, anyway. Why is God in your life if you won't let Him do for you? Let Him open the door and pull out your chair. Allow Him to be your personal chef. He's an awesome cook and right at this moment He is preparing a lavish table feast before you, of all your heart's desires, in the presence of your enemies, so all you have to do is sit back and relax. Stop doing all this running and just be still and know that He is God.

In 2 Corinthians 3:7 the Bible reads: "We go through to comfort and console others." As a young adult, I had the mindset that by age twenty-five, I was going to be doing such and such, no kids, my way or the highway, with prideful attitude, living it up. One day, living at the peak of invincible moments as most young people do, I became pregnant. My pregnancy was not planned. Yes, I had a job, an apartment, and a car, but I was not mentally, physically, or financially prepared to take care of a child when I had just begun to take care of myself. I was scared and embarrassed, and didn't know what to do. I felt ashamed that I been so careless after having been raised up in a God-fearing home. I knew this would hurt my mother deeply.

I remember going through the pregnancy tests, buying three of them hoping they would be negative, and later going to the doctor for confirmation. The doctor and staff were giving me all these congratulations, but I was not thrilled. After I convinced myself that this was really happening, I broke the news to my child's father. I met him for lunch and we were sitting in the car and I told him, "You're about to be a dad –again." He was silent for a while (I'm sure he was thinking he already had a kid and was paying child support on her behalf) and then he asked me, "What are *you* going to do about it? I'm cool with whatever you decide to do." I will never forget the feelings that transcended from his words for as long as I live. At that moment, I was fragranced in complete brokenness. One, he acted like I did this by myself; and two, I had always been pro-life, but I was faced with walking in a different pair of shoes, and I contemplated abortion for the entire first trimester.

I took responsibility for what I had done, and told the Lord I would give him (my child) back to Lord. I had a good pregnancy, no complications, and gave birth to a beautiful baby boy. I began to rejoice in the blessing that God didn't give me a barren womb, and in how beautiful it was to have life growing inside of me. Having my son changed my life—for the better. I was careless in my actions, but little did I know that God would turn my brokenness into blessings-- not just for me, but others I have come into contact with as well. God has brought into my life so many young women whom otherwise I would never have met, to help heal and encourage. That's when I count it all joy: the trials, the tears, and the heartache during my single motherhood thus far, because I have discovered the aromatic base note of brokenness as blessing.

Fragrance of Prayer

We have automatic coffee makers, central heating and air conditioning, cars that start automatically with the press of the start-stop button. We even have automated toilets that do the flushing for us. What luxury we live in! How automatic is our prayer life? The Bible tells us in 1 Thessalonians 5:17, we are to pray without ceasing. In Psalm 55:17, it says: "Evening and morning and at noon, I will pray...." We know Jesus to be a provider and a way-maker, but He's more than Savior. He is a great listener, but He is Lord and commands us to pray—regularly. Before your feet hit the floor and you begin your day, pray. Don't brush your teeth, wash your face, or unwrap your hair until you pray. Prayer should be as automatic as saying grace before you eat a meal. For me, I am praying in the car too. The people in the lane next to me may think I'm crazy because it looks like I'm talking to myself, but Jesus is riding with me wherever I go.

Prayer is nothing more than communicating with our Lord. What good is having a relationship with a significant other if you never talk to each other? I can recall being in a relationship, having a dinner in a nice restaurant, and the conversation was basically held on mute. All you could hear was the voices of neighboring table conversations and the sound of our silverware pinging the plates. This was not a time when silence was golden; it spoke volumes about how absolutely horrible the relationship was. There was nothing to say. Short and sweet, we were unequally yoked—going nowhere. I could smell the fragrance of Christ chastening me in my spirit, beckoning me, even though I was doing wrong. My prayer life at that time wasn't consistent, except for saying grace before I ate a meal, but nevertheless, His fragrance was drawing me in to seek His face.

I specifically remember one night after having made love to this man, I lay there with my back turned toward him in disgust while he was commenting on how good it was and asking me for my approval. If one knows they have fulfilled a responsibility without error, one need not ask for survey approval. I did not reply, being annoyed with him, yet angry with myself and feeling like I had bathed in manure, so I pretended to go to sleep. I had tears in my eyes from the weight of a heavy, broken heart. I thought I was grown, and believed that was what I wanted. I prayed to God, silently telling Him I didn't want to live like this anymore. No matter how good he can put it down, nor matter how much money you have in the bank, or the name brands you have in your wardrobe, life without Christ isn't life at all. Isn't it something how the Scent of a Desperate Woman is usually complimentary to the Cologne Good D, No Mind? This was not who I was. I prayed earnestly for God to rescue me and get me out. I felt so bad, so guilty of being drowned in my own lusts…all because my guard was down due to a faint prayer life; thus the enemy caught me slipping and walked through the door of my vulnerability.

As tears graced my pillow, I could smell the fragrant aroma of Christ's love and my tears flowed even faster knowing He was in the room with me in the midst of my shame, standing right there with open arms. I can tell you God heard my prayer and provided a way of escape. After that moment, despite a few hiccups, my prayer life began to increase and I began desiring God like He desired to have me. It took wearing the Scent of Brokenness, I then recognized the aroma of my perfume.

The Bible compares prayer to incense. Psalm 141: 2 reads: "Let my prayer be set before You as incense, the lifting up of my hands as the evening sacrifice." Incense, once lit, continues to rise and saturate the atmosphere. Let your fragrance of prayer rise steadfastly before Him and fill His nostrils.

Don't stop praying. Pray in the bed if you can't get on your knees. With kids and work, school and busy schedules…pray in the shower. The Bible tells us to pray without ceasing (1 Thessalonians5:17) and it doesn't have to be one of those supa-dupa prayers as long as the Mississippi either. Just don't stop. If you are concrete in Christ, please read and heed. For my absolutes, those who are eating Lamb and bread—pray the Word; you know how to do this. Bring back to His remembrance what He said. You have a right as a queen, a daughter of the Most High God, to decree and declare a thing to be so. If you are unsure how to do it, get hold of the Word. Seek Him, and ask

Him to show you how to pray, and He will. For any problem, any situation, go to the Word of God, and that will be the end of your confusion. The Word is the ultimate and final authority. Thank God for Momma and Daddy and the blessing of genuine friends who will shake you when the need arises, but God has the final say in the matter. Honestly, a lot of our stress comes from running in the flesh rather than walking in the Spirit. We want to go to everyone else for an answer that appeases our flesh, rather than putting on our big girl panties and adhering to His Word. Paraphrased, *"His thoughts are not your thoughts, and His ways are higher than your ways."* (Isaiah 55:18) Girl, stop stressing and let Him handle it. Of course I know it's easier said than done. I hear you saying, "You have no idea what I'm up against right now." I may not know the details of your issue, but I know who He is, and He has a plan. He will perfect those things concerning you and if faithful to complete the work in you until the day of Jesus Christ. (Philippians1:6) Be encouraged; everything is going to work out. Believe Him and trust Him.

In church we hear, "Honey, just wait on the Lord; He's going to turn it around--just wait on God. Weeping may endure for a night." Ooohhh, that's the one verse right there--hearing it so much, I became irritated by it. I'm thinking if another sister gets in my face, gives me that church hug and tells me that again, I'm gonna scream! I found myself yelling out of my spirit to the Lord, "I guess I have been in 'night' for years, when am I going to get a come up?! I don't see any relief." As a matter of fact, every time the slightest hint of relief is within my vicinity, it disappears and I end up taking two steps back. In my walk with Him, I have learned there is no way around it. You do have to wait, but it's *how* you wait that can determine the time of the breakthrough or blessing. I have learned He is his Word, so while you are waiting, here are two promises to hold on to:

The Lord spoke in Isaiah 55:11, "So shall My word be that goes forth from My mouth; It shall not return to Me void, But it shall accomplish what I please, and it shall prosper in the thing for which I have sent it. For you shall go out with joy, and be led out with peace." In Isaiah 46, God tells us, "Indeed I have spoken it; I will also bring it to pass. I have purposed it; I will also do it." Please keep in mind while you wear the Fragrance of Brokenness, it may be for the benefit of another to encourage, inspire, or restore on behalf of the glory of God.

Humility

First, let's talk about what it is not. Humility is not being a punk, contrary to popular opinion. Humility is not a weakness, and being humble is not a deficiency or disability. Being humble is a display of the utmost intangible strength one can possess. Fragrancing yourself with humility is taking the lowly place while you may indeed be more than qualified for the higher position.

When God sent His Son Jesus to sacrifice His life for ours, that was the epitome of humility. (John 3:16) It is shutting your mouth and not getting the last word. It's not prodding around with conceitedness and acting above another. Humility is to deny yourself and starve your ego. Woman-up and apologize. Forget how you look and what others will think of you. What matters is what God thinks of you. Being humble carries great reward in Christ. The top notes are of gentleness, while the heart notes grace this fragrance with suffering and light afflictions; the base note abounds with inheritance, honor, and esteem.

The world would have you believe you have to get yours first, like showing humility is displaying weakness. The meek shall inherit the earth. Being meek or humble does not mean you are a punk. I take the perspective of okay, I don't have to exert my energy on what is usually a trivial matter to get my point across. I'm gonna let you keep talking; you can go first or whatever it is because you keep talking crazy--you don't know who you are dealing with. My Father has the mentality "come with it" found in Isaiah 50:8. Be very careful of what you say and do to a child of God. I will pray for you and keep it moving, as the "Humble in spirit shall retain honor." (Proverbs 29:23) Ladies, having the last word to prove a point verbally, or indeed otherwise is not honorable. It's a pride and ego thing. You see it all the time in reality television. Foolishness and shame speak volumes alone. It takes a great woman to be humbled, to shut up, and let God be her God.

Early in my profession, I was done a grave injustice by a supervisor and her word became a permanent fixture on my performance record. I was very angry at that time and wanted to act out and be vengeful. I had her on my list, so to speak. It took a minute, but eventually, I just forgave and let it go. What was done, was done. About seven years later, I decided to contact her and ask if she had continuity to share on a certain subject I knew she was an expert in. Without regard to what happened in the past and me not bringing it up, she immediately apologized and explained how regretful she was about the incident that happened so many years ago. I was shocked to hear the words coming out of her mouth. I had forgotten about it. But it goes to show that because I humbled myself and did not retaliate or get my revenge from careless actions that may have ensued and cost me dearly, God had reaped burning coals on her head all this time.

Fragrancing yourself with humility, not seeking your own glory, but the glory of others, giving credit where it is due, taking the lowly place; it doesn't matter how you phrase it, God will see to it your humility is honored.

Restoration

Women who fancy this fragrance are natural givers who have tender, generous hearts filled with power of transformation by touch. They see beyond an individual's dress, circumstance, and smile. They have an innate desire to give their all to help others in need, and rightly do so when they are in need themselves. While everyone else has turned their back, the fragrance of restoration motivates the wearer to bring change for the better and see the good past the bad in others, awakening those affected by the sleep of idleness. Ladies of this scent are full of compassion and servitude. They have an attitude of "I'm going to help you get back on your feet, what do you need me to do? I'm not focused on where you are now, but where you are going? How can I help you become better?" Restoration has the fixatives of mercy and grace within it. Although their kindness in word and deed are often taken for granted or abused, those affected by the women who wear this fragrance never forget acts of kindness given to them-- these gracious women who aid in helping to restore others retain honor. (Proverbs 11:16) Women are fragranced with restoration indeed have hearts after God. They see and understand the heart of man as God does.

Sound Mind

A sound mind is one at peace within herself. I learned a long time ago that worrying doesn't do it for me. I have learned to acknowledge and dismiss quickly if this situation or person will potentially disrupt my sound mind. I'm too old to allow a situation or person mess with my peace. I enjoy my beauty rest and if I'm up worried and can't sleep, that's not good for anyone within my vicinity. I cannot allow you to disturb my peace. I need to keep a sound mind. Without it, I am distracted and bring upon myself the inability to have sober thinking against Satan or his minions in the strategies to deter my focus on what's really going on. With whatever decision I make, best believe I'm going to sleep at night. I have learned that when I am operating with a sound mind, I make sober decisions and I am more physically relaxed. I am able to hear Jesus with clarity. C'mon now, if God isn't worried about it, why should you be? After I have prayed and have stood on His word…it is what it is. Lord, let Your will be done.

The wearer of this signature fragrance will not be afraid, for God did not give her a spirit of fear, but of love, power and sound mind.

What can man do to her? This fragrance endows the wearer not to be afraid of what man can do, but to be fearful of the one who can put both body and soul in hell. The perfumista of this scent is at peace with others and herself. Note to self: As a Perfumed Letter, when you are not at peace, you are frantic and restless, and your letter crumbles. When the letter crumbles, no one can see strength of what is written inside. The scent may be there, but the words are not legible. Thus, she rocks this fragrance whenever the need arises, especially in the case of much-needed beauty sleep…it is a lavender-scented smoothie, allowing her to rest with peace of mind in any given situation.

Fierce Faith

A woman who fragrances herself with Fierce Faith is immovable and unstoppable. She knows without a doubt, she has been given a kingdom that cannot be shaken. Despite the pressing and temporal chaos surrounding her, she continues to believe in the power of what she cannot see with the natural eyes, and against all odds, sprays this fragrance on to create those things that she cannot see with physical eyes into tangible glories. Fierce faith revitalizes you in weakness, and warrants you to keep pushing to see what the end will be. By this faith we are justified and have peace that surpasses all understanding, guarding our hearts and minds in Christ Jesus.

The fragrance propels her from glory to glory in Christ Jesus, because she has ride or die faith. She comes boldly to the throne, believing that He is, and no one or nothing can tell her different. It's more than materialistic, it is the synergy between her and her Lord. She possesses a faith so fierce that she is "Persuaded that neither death nor life, nor angels, nor principalities nor powers, nor things to come, nor height nor depth, nor any other created thing, shall be able to separate her from the love of God which is in Christ Jesus her Lord." (Romans 8:38-39)

Love

While all of the aforementioned scents are wonderful in their own right, the greatest of these is love. Perfect love casts out fear. It covers all wrongdoings--and I'm not talking about bad breath or betrayal in any form. Love covers every molestation, rape, murder, and abuse. I am not referring to like, but love. Oooohhh, it is rather difficult to fathom, but let's be real. It's difficult only because our flesh makes it that way. Those that worship Him, must worship Him in spirit and in truth, right? The truth: God is love, are we?

God is love. The Bible tells us in Ephesians 3:19 that we are "to know the love of Christ which passes knowledge, that [we] may be filled with all the fullness of God." Italics mine. That kind of "know" is an intimate know. There is nothing casual about it. Meditate on that, ladies. Since before you were delicately placed in your mother's womb until now, as independent and co-dependent on God, He has loved you with a love beyond human comprehension--which is why we love Him, because He first loved us. We know it in this earthly realm as unconditional love and forgiveness. Spiritually, I believe this love looks beyond the spirit hovering over that person and pierces the heart of that individual. Could this be why Jesus prayed to God on the cross, asking Him to forgive them (us) for they know not what they do? Jesus was loving, like His Father, in THE MOST DIFFICULT MOMENT OF HIS LIFE—reaching past outer appearances and all acts we would ever do, but looked at His love for us. We all are spirit-controlled...but by who, is the question? If we can grasp His understanding in our spirits, we will be filled with the fullness of Him. We will be able to authentically love people who do not look like us, who do not share our faith or cultured values. Loving like Him, we will be able to show the same exceeding riches of grace and kindness He has bestowed upon us. Really, can you, will you seek to know the love of Christ?

Reflection: What's your signature fragrance? It may not be one that is listed above in this chapter, but what is that one scent that a person can smell to readily identify or associate you with a mile away, knowing without doubt that you must be in building? Which fragrances would you like to try? Not sure? Pray about it. God will let you know which fragrance is appropriate to wear at this moment.

Black Market Scents

"Lest Satan should take advantage of us; for we are not ignorant of his devices." (2 Corinthians 2:11)

Many perfumes, although they may initially smell sweet from the impression of a top note, will later catch you off guard as oppressive when the top and heart notes fade. These perfumes can cause spiritual health and environmental problems when used by wrong motives, or when abused in substantial qualities giving way to headaches (not thinking straight), allergic reactions (i.e. repelling blessings), nausea (vomiting, only to return to mess), affecting not only the end user, but all who are within reach.

When we say, "she makes me sick," or "ugh, she has such a stank attitude," literally, that may indeed be true by the scent she is wearing...or it could be you're being fragranced with the wrong scent. Why? How could you possibly be fragranced incorrectly if she is the one with the stank attitude? One, check yourself. If you are wearing a discontinued or not-ready-yet anointing and have busied yourself with a fragrance line you created without God's seal of approval by the blood of Christ (because it seemed like the right thing to do), whatever scents there may be will eventually bring death (Proverbs 14:12) I'm not saying that to be mean--I'm a realist, and that's the Bible. I mean really, doesn't it bother you when after a long day of face-to- face contact with everyone from co-workers to the grocery cashier and waitress at the restaurant that you find out when you arrive home, you have a peek-a-boo booger or sleep in your eyes or that your breath was popping in the wrong way but no one offered up a mint or something? Ugh! Why didn't anyone tell you? No, I'm not going to sugarcoat it for you. Sometimes our stuff stinks, and out of love, we need someone to tell us about ourselves. The point is a woman out of position or place is usually the result of a badly preserved fragrance--and God does not want that for you.

Scent of a Desperate Woman

I find it amazing how scents can catch you off guard, chauffeur you down memory lane and evoke a range of emotions from 0-60 in two seconds. Scents have such power to bring out the good and the stupid in people. Frowned upon, this scent is extremely popular among the young and old, and is sadly considered a best-seller among the weakest to the strongest of us. It does not discriminate. This scent can be applied to anyone under the right circumstances: job, career, money, marriage, children. One such perfume is the Scent of a Desperate Woman. The Bible reviews this fragrance like this: "To a hungry soul, every bitter thing is sweet." (Proverbs 27:7) Men and women alike can smell this a mile away. While the presentation of the package may be flamboyant and sexy, the effect of this scent breeds heartache and utter devastation. We all know a woman who wears this scent. It may be that you have even had this particular fragrance in your collection once upon a time. This scent causes a woman to run without caution (feet are not at home) and turn a deaf ear to wisdom and integrity.

I announce to you do not purchase, nor try a dab of it on! Whoever told you it smells great on you, lied to you. It is not cute for a daughter of the Most High to be chasing after a mortal man or anything else materialistically. We have been seated together in heavenly places with Jesus, as said in Ephesians 2:6. When have you ever heard of royalty chasing after anything in acts of desperation? Our God supplies all of our needs according to His riches in glory; thus, whatever it is you are trying to obtain by desperate measures, you don't need it. His job as a parent is to provide you with three things: shelter, food, and clothes. You have a mansion, you have the Word of God (bread), and the Lamb of God (Jesus) for food. You have a garment of praise for the spirit of heaviness, and the sandals of the gospel of peace--which also come in sneakers, stilettos, sandals, and boots--for whatever terrain you encounter on your walk with Him. Anything else, like a blessing here or there, and favor, is extra. "God things" --not just good things--come to those who wait. Despite the lovely presentation in the bottle, the aroma acts as a repellant (of blessing and divine favor). While you believe you are attracting "the one," "the deal," or "the house loan," the scent is tearing away at your character and raping your self-worth and dignity. This scent will do more collateral damage than good as it affects everyone around you. As the fragrance seeps through your pulse points, it will intensify, linger, and eventually produce a foul odor.

The Bible makes it clear that you must not be anxious for anything. "In everything let prayer and supplications be made known before God and the peace of God that surpasses all understanding will guard your heart and mind in Christ Jesus." (Philippians 4:7) Where the thoughts of your mind go, covered or not, your body will follow. It doesn't matter what you are desperate for—seeking the approval of a parent, recognition from the boss, significance from a man or children, the title that comes with the ring or degree, STOP IT! If you are looking for significance from anyone or anything other God, you have made them your god. If they don't know who they are, what standard do they have to measure you and tell you who you are supposed to be? None. Your standard is the Word of God.

As women, we have been given the power of influence, the ability to bring forth nations, and when we put on this fragrance, people get hurt and dreams are shattered. The Bible talks about what happens when women wear the Scent of a Desperate Woman. Ready? Go with me to Isaiah 44: 9-20 to break it down.

We all have learned or at least have heard the commandment, "Thou shalt have no other gods before me." Let's begin. "Those who make an image, all of them are useless...." [the image the Word is referring to here is the graven images, images of gods we place ahead of the true and living God.] "And their precious things shall not profit. They are their own witness." In Proverbs 18:1, we find that "a man who isolates himself sets his own desire; he rages against all use of judgment." Ladies, we fall into trouble when we are led away by our own desires.

Let's get something straight; God didn't make you do it, and Satan didn't either. When you say, "Oh, the devil made me do it," you are giving him too much credit. All he did was offer up a suggestion, whispering something sweet you know you wanted to hear. It's not a good look to want (you fill in the blank) so bad that you lust for it. Desiring something is not bad; lusting after it is. When you make people or material things your god, placing it before God, you will eventually run into trouble and drama. God says in His word that He will withhold no good thing (Psalm 84:11) from us. He may say, "Not yet," but we withhold those good things from ourselves. (Jeremiah 5:25)

Wearing the Scent of a Desperate Woman involves our own iniquities. So why is it you're not blessed or favored and receiving the promises? Check your scent, honey, and if it's the Scent of a Desperate Woman, trash it. Verse 9 continued: "They neither see nor know that they may be ashamed." Verse 10: "Who would form a god or mold an image that profits him nothing?" The essence of what this fragrance is, is noted in Matthew 16:26. "For what profit is it to a man if He gains the whole world, and loses his own soul? Or what will a man give in exchange for his soul?"

For example, you consciously know this man is wrapped up in an enticing piece of artwork, but when you are rocking this black market scent, you lose sight of who you are in Christ and cannot look at him unbiased. You fail to notice the fact while his sex game is amazing, he is honestly unavailable relationally, and so are you in that moment, yet living with you sounds like a viable option for him. You know this man isn't going to do you (or your kids if they apply to the situation) any good. Because you are desperate, your focus is completely off, so tell me…is your mentality 1) having a man is better than no man at all 2) having dick in your life is better than none at all or 3) this is part of my game plan consciously or sub-consciously to get him saved or wait with him to make a decision to marry me? Yes, I am addressing the believer. Ladies, we can go tit for tat on this. Yes, I said it, and? Desperate to fit in, we wear clothes not made for our silhouettes, in which our vaginas can't breathe, spend money foolishly so children can't eat, or we try to be beautiful but can't get past pretty's deception. We put on the church face, but we struggle as soon as we get on the church parking lot. What is it that you are so willing to get (fill in the blank) that you lose yourself over? (Matthew 16:26) Attention? A few minutes of pleasure? Cash money? A title? An orgasm? Friends? If you're reading this and you are Hallelujah-Holy-Ghost-filled, speaking-in-tongues saved, claiming Christ as your Lord and savior, go find a prayer closet, because if I have just described you, it's time to go scrub this scent off, washing it in the blood of Jesus.

Okay, your issue is not a man. Could it be you have such a lust to get this money or to climb the career ladder that you want this position so bad, you step over co-workers, dismissing interpersonal relationships with friends, hurting them in the process just to get a the lights, camera, action or the orgasm for a moment? Be careful. Again, it is not wrong to desire, but once your desire becomes bigger than Jesus and you find yourself laying down your life for it--girl, this is a major problem! You can't be whole, yet halfway desperate? This scent is one of many tailored by Satan and his team of experts in the fields designed to steal, kill, and destroy your life and purpose.

Desperation is also known as people-pleasing--mind you, I said people pleasing, not God-pleasing. People-pleasing involves constantly breaking your back and being a yes-woman to get approval of a mortal or object. Desperation is acting out of fear, rather than faith, worrying in place of worshipping. The motto is: "I don't want to wait, I'll do it myself."

The Scent of a Desperate Woman is a fragrance that repels patience. When you do not wait, you cannot be made perfect. "But let patience have its perfect work, that you may be perfect and complete, lacking nothing." (James 1:4) To be desperate is to lack something. Desperation has an all-or-nothing attitude and wants what it wants at any cost. Wearing this scent will cost you to lose yourself and your purpose.

Verse 11: "Surely all his companions would be ashamed." Hopefully, you have surrounded yourself with good friends and family who will get in your face and shake you if need be.

Verse 12: Pay particular attention to the middle portion of the verse: "And it works with the strength of His arms." Notice the verse says "His arms," not God's. We are strong in the Lord and in the power of His might. When you lavish yourself with this fragrance, you become weak and fragile, but there is good news. In Romans

8:26, we find the Spirit helps in our weakness. His strength is made perfect in our weakness. (2 Corinthians 12:9) Being weak and without strength leads to foolish decisions you wouldn't otherwise make if you were sober in your thinking.

Verse 13: "The craftsman stretches out his rule." Reading verse 13 in its entirety, you will see that the craftsman is cunning and smart, laying out a blueprint, a specific plan for her prey. She intricately designs the specifications of how she wants her man—tall, money, kid-free, and straight teeth. He can't have Mister's attitude about women. Isaiah said [she] "makes it like," meaning trying to come close to what she thinks she needs and wants. It goes on to say in Verse 13—"according to the beauty of a man" (not the beauty of the Lord). This scent in any fashion—body wash or lotion--will bring sorrow. I have seen beautifully decorated yet desperate women (I used to be one of them) that were utterly stank because of this fragrance. You know who you are. The Scent of a Desperate Woman does not wear off easily.

Remember your clubbing days, going through the motions of getting so fresh and clean, dolled up and sexy-as-ever, smelling good, only to come home smelling like smoke? Ugh! Take a minute to reflect on this "Oh yes, and amen" flashback. Looking back, it was just foolish. Go out smelling like Dove® and Bodyshop® to return home smelling of cigarettes and weed, all in your nicely relaxed wash, set, and style.

How can we get rid of this scent? Go take a bath or a shower, spiritually speaking. (Psalm 24:4-5) "He who has clean hands and a pure heart who does not lift up his soul to an idol or swear by what is false. He will receive a blessing from the Lord and vindication from God His Savior." What is the motive? Why do you want whatever it is so badly? You're right, God does know your heart, but do you?

Verse 15: Listen to this. "Then it shall be for a man to burn. For he will take some of it and warm himself [lust of your desperation];

yes, he kindles it [arouses it--lust] and bakes bread. Indeed he makes a god and worships it; He makes it a carved image with diligent effort and concentration." Whenever you worship idols, you exert a great amount of energy, putting forth devotion in something that does not advance the kingdom. When you worship someone other than God, you relinquish your perfume and the power within, giving the enemy full reign over your anointing.

Pay special attention to what happens after you have taken time to carve your image—you fall down to it. Praise interruption: a righteous man may fall seven times, but he will rise again.

Verse 16: "He burns half of it [with eyes bigger than his stomach] and [temporarily] satisfied." In our terms: Halfway in I can change him, halfway out I can get him saved. I'll pay half of my tithes this month because God knows my heart. "He even warms himself and says, 'Ah! I am warm,' I have seen [internalized] the fire [consumption]." What happened was that after your eyes became bigger than your stomach, you found out the truth of the matter and were deceived. You were led to believe to you were being comforted, while simultaneously confused. The reality is that you see what you want to see right now, and nobody can tell you anything. You have allowed the enemy to put a veil over your eyes.

Verse 17: "And the rest of it he makes into a god and worships it. Prays to it and says, Deliver me, for you are my god!" I'm shaking my head, because I have been there. I have made a man my god. I have made money my god. The Scent of a Desperate Woman will have you seeking deliverance from whatever it is you are lusting after. Get rid of this scent and listen to wisdom. See Proverbs 5:3-6, 8-13.

Allergic Reactions

Keep purchasing this fragrance if you want to. God said in Psalm 81:12, "He will give you to your heart to walk in your own counsel led by your own desire." If you are wearing the scent, check the below symptoms and allergic reactions and please consult the Physician if they occur.

- Spiritual bipolarity, also known by the Physician as "being lukewarm," as in, on fire for Christ one minute and doing your own thing the next. (Revelation 3:16)
- Dry mouth/saltiness, also known as regret. (Genesis 19:26)
- Vomiting, or returning to foolishness you have been delivered from. (Proverbs 26:11)
- Hallucinations/believing the lies of the enemy. (John 8:44)
- Worry warts, or encompassing yourself in fear rather than faith. (Matthew 6:25-34)
- Acute dishonor, or throwing your pearls before swine. (Matthew 7:6)
- Malnourishment, or diminished character. (Matthew 4:4)
- Decreased self-worth, including whoring after people and things that devalue you. (Psalm 6:26)

I am a firm believer that God will meet you where you are. He will restore. If this is a matter of being unequally yoked, God will not do it for you. He will provide a way of escape, for He is our refuge, but you are going to have to move your feet to get there. You are going to have to make a move. He promised in His word that if you separate yourself from an unbeliever, He will treat you kindly and with favor. He will not leave you hanging, as though you didn't get yours in this relationship. Begin to worship Him in spirit and in truth, and you will recognize that you don't have to be desperate for anything. He will supply all of your needs according to His riches and glory, and the desires of your heart as well, upon certain conditions. I know from experience how exhausting wearing this fragrance can be, but Jesus said, "Come to me all you who labor and are heavy laden and I will give you rest." (Matthew 11:28, NKJV) He said you don't have to be anxious, but pray--pray believing, asking--and He will give it to you. What can we do to rid ourselves of such a stinking and foul odor? We must repent, and rededicate our lives as believers, and be content with whatever state we find ourselves in.

Drama Queen

This fragrance is as loud as it can be strong. Usually the woman who wears it is an attention-seeker. It doesn't matter if the attention is good or bad, as long as she gets the attention. This scent causes the wearer to be very conniving and manipulative. Intrigued by problems and conflict other than her own, she is her own reality show, out front and theatrical in the worst way. She loathes in being in the middle of mess, shifting blame, instigating or switching sides when it is convenient for her, and in her best interest only, without regard to the damage she can cause. If you don't watch the company you keep and a woman within your circle of friends indirectly states this is her favorite, the scent will rub off on you. Unless you are a "violent Christian woman" (Matthew 11:12) taking something back from the enemy, this scent is rather unpleasant in the sight of God and man. The heart note of this fragrance is division, to overreact or respond poorly to a given situation, forsaking being "swift to hear, slow to speak and slow to wrath." (James 1:19) There is no correlation between the scent of Drama Queen and age, as it can happen at any time. When women wear Drama Queen, they forget the power of their influence and indeed affect hundreds if not thousands of other women.

Pride

The scent of pride is not one that God likes at all. Acts Chapter 5:1-10, NIV

> 1: Now a man named Ananias, together with his wife Sapphira, also sold a piece of property. 2 With his wife's full

knowledge he kept back part of the money for himself, but brought the rest and put it at the apostles' feet.

3: Then Peter said, "Ananias, how is it that Satan has so filled your heart that you have lied to the Holy Spirit and have kept for yourself some of the money you received for the land? 4 Didn't it belong to you before it was sold? And after it was sold, wasn't the money at your disposal? What made you think of doing such a thing? You have not lied just to human beings but to God."

5: When Ananias heard this, he fell down and died. And great fear seized all who heard what had happened. 6 Then some young men came forward, wrapped up his body, and carried him out and buried him.

7: About three hours later his wife came in, not knowing what had happened. 8 Peter asked her, "Tell me, is this the price you and Ananias got for the land?"
"Yes," she said, "that is the price."

9: Peter said to her, "How could you conspire to test the Spirit of the Lord? Listen! The feet of the men who buried your husband are at the door, and they will carry you out also."

10: At that moment she fell down at his feet and died. Then the young men came in and, finding her dead, carried her out and buried her beside her husband.

Isn't that something, how when prideful individuals get caught, they "die" of embarrassment because they have been publicly humiliated? (Proverbs 11:2) It's one thing to be proud of an accomplishment or goal reached and you are the only person who knows, but it is another matter when you take credit and build yourself a pedestal and homemade tiara, looking down upon others. Have no fear. God loves you still, but He hates the pride, and you can look forward to falling from the same pedestal you so energetically built for yourself--just saying. (Proverbs 16:18) It is God and His grace who gives you the breath in your body and second chances in the tens of thousands, so be happy about your achievement and celebrate, but always remain humble.

Envy

Who can stand before jealousy? Not even God. (Exodus 20:4-5) It is that serious. Let's bring it down to our level. Your perfume is worth more than the material possessions and trinkets of another could ever be. Look at it from this perspective. Her (the woman you are envious of) anointing took 17,301 petals and 3700 pressings for each individual one. Yours will only take 15,301 petals and 3699 pressings just to make an ounce of perfumed oil. Being envious will stifle your originality and make you into a copy. Use the word of God as a mirror, not another woman.

I speak from experience, ladies. This scent is a prelude to bitterness. I remember I had it seeping through my pores so bad, I couldn't watch a simple movie. It was absolutely pitiful. The envy gave way to insecurity, making me incoherent, clouding my judgment, and weakening my spiritual immune system of who I was in Christ. This fragrance is not lovely at all. Envy can literally rot your body from the inside out. The Word says, in James 3:16, that a host of unnecessary drama appears wherever there is envy.

YOUR perfume is consecrated and expensive, thus YOUR worth is far above rubies. (Proverbs 31:10) Being envious will do nothing but sour your scent, so mirror yourself in the Word, rather than in what someone else has. On that same note, Paul tells us in 1 Thessalonians 4:11 to mind our own business and work with our own hands. The only time you get envious of another is when you are idle, not minding your own business and counting your own blessings, and that foolishness will eventually tear down your own house. (Proverbs 14:1) Seriously, if you are wearing this fragrance, go exfoliate yourself in the Word and make a list of blessings you can praise God for.

Infared

There is nothing wrong with being angry if you keep your anger in check. The Word of God tells us to be angry, but sin not and do not let the sun go down on your wrath.

A queen in the Bible named Athaliah made anger her signature scent. The grave tragedy of losing her husband and having to bury her young son was what caused it. She then took her anger to another level and faithfully tried to compensate for her losses by seeking power through evil and violence. The anger numbed her till this lady even tried to kill her own grandson. I am so serious. The Bible says that after her losses, "she proceeded to destroy the whole royal family of the house of Judah." She let the sun go down on her wrath, and her anger consumed her. You can find her story in 2 Chronicles 22: 10-12 and 2 Chronicles 23.

I remember not so long ago, I was a very angry woman from the time I woke up till the time I went to sleep, and then had the audacity to be mad at myself for being angry. Yes, I was still a professing Christian, but the only thing that made me happy was my son, Fridays when the clock hit 4:00 in the afternoon, good sex, and payday. Yes, I said it. I'm trying to be transparent with you. Let the real be recognized. I could pray when I got up and ate a little bit of Word, but by the time I showed up to work, the spirit of anger had control of me. I allowed the enemy to plague me with my past hurts of everything from my father not being in my life, to having a child out of wedlock, to relationships in which I was used for gain—a receptacle and nothing else--on repeat, on top of that. My anger had lasted for so long, I didn't even know why I was angry anymore. Angry people are hurting people, and need love that covers all wrongs. I didn't want to be angry, it just became who I was. I knew I needed help and I knew where my help would come from. Despite my distance from the Lord, He never distanced Himself from me. I sought the Lord wholeheartedly by praying, making sufficient time to get in His Word on a daily basis and making a conscious effort nearly every hour of the day to bring my flesh under the subjection in Christ with the Word. As I write to you, I have been delivered! If you are angry, pray, work out your own salvation; seek the Lord, and count your blessings.

Reflection: None of the aforementioned scents is lovely for a Daughter of the King to wear. If indeed you are wearing one of them, go exfoliate yourself in the Word and allow Jesus to cleanse you as soon as possible. Confess it, for He is faithful and just to forgive you and cleanse you from all unrighteousness.

Synthetic Fragrances

"Better to be a nobody and yet have...than pretend to be a somebody and have no food." (Proverbs 12:9)

Synthetic perfumes are bootleg copies of the original worn by women known as pretenders and superficialists (yes, I just made up that word).

Anything that is synthetic is a duplicate of the original. It is usually a cheaper, alternate version of the real thing, composed of poor-quality materials or ingredients, and it evaporates quickly. Merriam-Webster's dictionary defines synthetic as: "devised, arranged, or fabricated for special situations to imitate or replace usual realities; factitious, bogus." Synthetic fragrances are known to be liars, deceivers of the truth, and collaborators with the accuser of the brethren.

Let's mark the list:

- Fake hair
- Fake eye color
- Fake breasts
- Fake lips
- Fake booty
- Fake skin complexion
- Fake nails

I guess I forgot to make mention of the fake hearts and fake praise. I'm not judging nor knocking any of the items mentioned above (I rock my wigs sometimes and a push-up every now and again too), but my point is there's a lot of phoniness, a lot of perfumistas rocking cheap perfume and fragrances in the body of Christ. When I say cheap, I mean it costs them nothing to be superficial. It is one matter to be cordial and polite as a lady, treating others with the same respect as you would to yourself and loving your neighbor as yourself, but it's entirely another matter to be outright phony. My question to you is: If Jesus is real, why can't you be? Many individuals are pretending to be the head, while they are indeed the hip bone, while others are pretending to be eyes instead of ears and fingers instead of toes. I'm not talking about those who have backslid or those who have simply made a mistake or two or ten and sought repentance. I am referring to those who are one pedicured foot in and one pedicured foot out whenever it is convenient for the occasion. The Bible graciously titles them "lukewarm" Christians.

There is no use in trying to be something you were not created to be. I speak from experience when I tell you it's a waste of time. The woman in the next cubicle has her own unique perfume; your child's teacher and the waitress at your favorite restaurant has her own divine fragrance as well. Why are you so concerned with this other woman's body features or her personality? Is it really that important for you to compare yourself with the likes of another, working feverishly to get her anointing and having the nerve to ask God to give you "her" anointing? I mean, every time you see her or someone like her, you frown and catch an attitude or have something negative to say. Stop! Let me emphasize, you cannot be replicated or duplicated, and neither can she.

Ladies, my objective in the writing of this book is not to belittle, nor to flatter you. It is make you aware of the truth and remind you that you may want to change your current fragrance wardrobe for what He bought you. The problem is that no one has told you your stuff stinks and because I love you, I'm going to tell you the truth: Every fragrance and perfume does not smell right on everybody, and wearing the fragrance of Pretty Pretender stinks. Indeed, the perfume smelled wonderful on her. You were thinking it would suit you too, and so you complimented her and inquired where you could purchase it, but was not forewarned it may not be the best scent for you.

Pretty Pretender

We are going to have a conversation about three women in the Bible who casually wore the fragrance Pretty Pretender, and discuss the repercussions of this scent.

PERFUMISTA: WIFE OF JEROBOAM

We can find her story in the book of 1 Kings 14:1-17, NIV.

1   At that time Abijah son of Jeroboam became ill,
2   and Jeroboam said to his wife, "Go, disguise yourself, so you won't be recognized as the wife of Jeroboam. Then go to Shiloh. Ahijah the prophet is there—the one who told me I would be king over this people.
3   Take ten loaves of bread with you, some cakes and a jar of honey, and go to him. He will tell you what will happen to the boy."

4   So Jeroboam's wife did what he said and went to Ahijah's house in Shiloh. Now Ahijah could not see; his sight was gone because of his age.

5   But the LORD had told Ahijah, "Jeroboam's wife is coming to ask you about her son, for he is ill, and you are to give her such and such an answer. When she arrives, she will pretend to be someone else."

6   So when Ahijah heard the sound of her footsteps at the door, he said, "Come in, wife of Jeroboam. Why this pretense? I have been sent to you with bad news.

7   Go, tell Jeroboam that this is what the LORD, the God of Israel, says: 'I raised you up from among the people and appointed you ruler over my people Israel.

8   I tore the kingdom away from the house of David and gave it to you, but you have not been like my servant David, who kept my commands and followed me with all his heart, doing only what was right in my eyes.

9   You have done more evil than all who lived before you. You have made for yourself other gods, idols made of metal; you have aroused my anger and turned your back on me.

10   "'Because of this, I am going to bring disaster on the house of Jeroboam. I will cut off from Jeroboam every last male in Israel—slave or free. I will burn up the house of Jeroboam as one burns dung, until it is all gone.

11   Dogs will eat those belonging to Jeroboam who die in the city, and the birds will feed on those who die in the country. The LORD has spoken!'

12   "As for you, go back home. When you set foot in your city, the boy will die. 13 All Israel will mourn for him and bury him. He is the only one belonging to Jeroboam who will be buried, because he is the only one in the house of Jeroboam in whom the LORD, the God of Israel, has found anything good.

14 "The LORD will raise up for himself a king over Israel who will cut off the family of Jeroboam. Even now this is beginning to happen.

15 And the LORD will strike Israel, so that it will be like a reed swaying in the water. He will uproot Israel from this good land that he gave to their ancestors and scatter them beyond the Euphrates River, because they aroused the LORD's anger by making Asherah poles.

16 And he will give Israel up because of the sins Jeroboam has committed and has caused Israel to commit."

17 Then Jeroboam's wife got up and left and went to Tirzah. As soon as she stepped over the threshold of the house, the boy died.

We learn from the beginning of this story that she is a wife, and the mother of a sick child. Her husband tells her to go to the man of God, the prophet Ahijah, to get a prescription, a word about their ill son, when his underlying motive was to have her inquire about his "promised" political position, his dream. Before she arrived, God had already gave the prophet a heads up about her visit to see him and the reason why, noting that she would come as a pretender. God knew who she was and was not all at taken by surprise. The man of God called her out on it, spoke the word as directed, and she went about her way.

I wonder if she knew disguising herself was the wrong thing to do. I am curious to know if she was a passive woman or if she even wanted to speak to her husband about it first. Did she pretend because she wanted to try God, or did she pretend to be another woman on behalf of her sick child? Notice that when she was asked, "Why are you pretending?" she said nothing. There was nothing to say. Was she going place blame on her husband, on the devil for making her do it? To pretend is to lie, to make believe. His Word clearly tells us to put away lying. What excuses if any, as a child of God, do you have to wear the Pretty Pretender fragrance?

I get it. Admittedly, we get tired of being pressed and refined for the umpteenth time and we have the inclination to put on Pretty Pretender in that moment of weakness. We will worry, put God in a box, and make it do what it do on our own. When we pretend to be another woman, independent of Him, we put in a lot of work exerting unnecessary energy on behalf of the enemy. Whether you are a believer in Christ or not, we will all give an account of the deeds done in the body--so sister, do yourself a favor and don't act brand new, fragrancing yourself with Pretty Pretender as if God cannot see you when you turn off the lights, change your voice or your spiritual stance. If God uses the earth as his footstool, do you really believe He can't see what you're doing? C'mon--let's get real, perfumista.

Why do you engage in gossip when you know you have been set apart from this foolishness? Why are you ashamed of Me when you are in public place, out with your girls, or your man, but you pretend to know Me when you need something? Why do you shut down and get hush when an opportunity is presented to you to share the good news of salvation? Why do you quickly listen to the advice or resolve of others and yet beckon to My wisdom and counsel as a last resort? Why are you acting like a peasant instead of a royal princess? I love you. I designed you and created a fabulous perfume all your own. Trust in Me. I am real and I need you to be as well.

PERFUMISTA: WOMAN OF TEKOA

Her theatrical debut can be found in 2 Samuel 14:1-20, NIV

1   Joab son of Zeruiah knew that the king's heart longed for Absalom.

2   So Joab sent someone to Tekoa and had a wise woman brought from there. He said to her, "Pretend you are in

mourning. Dress in mourning clothes, and don't use any cosmetic lotions. Act like a woman who has spent many days grieving for the dead.

3   Then go to the king and speak these words to him." And Joab put the words in her mouth.

4   When the woman from Tekoa went to the king, she fell with her face to the ground to pay him honor, and she said, "Help me, Your Majesty!"

5   The king asked her, "What is troubling you?"
    She said, "I am a widow; my husband is dead.

6   I your servant had two sons. They got into a fight with each other in the field, and no one was there to separate them. One struck the other and killed him.

7   Now the whole clan has risen up against your servant; they say, 'Hand over the one who struck his brother down, so that we may put him to death for the life of his brother whom he killed; then we will get rid of the heir as well.' They would put out the only burning coal I have left, leaving my husband neither name nor descendant on the face of the earth."

8   The king said to the woman, "Go home, and I will issue an order in your behalf."

9   But the woman from Tekoa said to him, "Let my lord the king pardon me and my family, and let the king and his throne be without guilt."

10 The king replied, "If anyone says anything to you, bring them to me, and they will not bother you again."

11 She said, "Then let the king invoke the LORD his God to prevent the avenger of blood from adding to the destruction, so that my son will not be destroyed."
    "As surely as the LORD lives," he said, "not one hair of your son's head will fall to the ground."

12   Then the woman said, "Let your servant speak a word to my
      lord the king."
      "Speak," he replied.

13   The woman said, "Why then have you devised a thing like
      this against the people of God? When the king says this,
      does he not convict himself, for the king has not brought
      back his banished son? 14 Like water spilled on the ground,
      which cannot be recovered, so we must die. But that is not
      what God desires; rather, he devises ways so that a banished
      person does not remain banished from him.

15   "And now I have come to say this to my lord the king because
      the people have made me afraid. Your servant thought, 'I will
      speak to the king; perhaps he will grant his servant's request.

16   Perhaps the king will agree to deliver his servant from the
      hand of the man who is trying to cut off both me and my son
      from God's inheritance.'

17   "And now your servant says, 'May the word of my lord the
      king secure my inheritance, for my lord the king is like an
      angel of God in discerning good and evil. May the LORD
      your God be with you.'"

18   Then the king said to the woman, "Don't keep from me the
      answer to what I am going to ask you."
      "Let my lord the king speak," the woman said.

19   The king asked, "Isn't the hand of Joab with you in all this?"
      The woman answered, "As surely as you live, my lord the
      king, no one can turn to the right or to the left from anything
      my lord the king says. Yes, it was your servant Joab who in-
      structed me to do this and who put all these words into the
      mouth of your servant.

20   Your servant Joab did this to change the present situation.
      My lord has wisdom like that of an angel of God—he knows
      everything that happens in the land."

The Bible says the Woman of Tekoa was wise, but just like you and me, she happened to have a dumb moment listening to a voice that did not belong to Jesus.

A few things to note in the text:

1. She was a wise woman.
2. She dressed in different clothing and makeup (changed her wardrobe and cosmetics).
3. She acted like a different woman (so animated in body language and theatrical in tears).
4. She let her guard down. Her words not her own, were put in her mouth from the manipulative spirit within Joab.
5. She lied and placed blame on others, said the people had made her afraid, specifically calling out Joab that he had commanded her and put the words in her mouth.

Ms. Tekoa fragranced herself with Pretty Pretender on behalf of someone else, as did Mrs. Jeroboam. However, Ms. Tekoa had some integrity (noted as a wise woman) and owned up to her lie when asked by the king why she was pretending—in other words, who had put her up to this. You will also notice within this story that she became engulfed in her new character of a different woman, stroking the king's ego throughout the text while playing on his emotions. Mrs. Jeroboam was married and had a baby. Ms. Tekoa was a single woman who pretended to have had a family at one time. What other differences can you note between the two women? Why are their stories relevant to us today?

Reflection: Pretty Pretender is not a flattering scent to be worn as a woman of God. We cannot advance the kingdom pretending to be someone else. As women of God, sanctified and righteous not by our works, (2 Corinthians 5:21) but by His power, this Pretty Pretender scent isn't us. Instead pretending to be delivered, walk in your deliverance--you have it already! Follow your own dreams, wear your own perfume; don't even attempt to borrow another woman's fragrance, for you have no idea of the pressing she went through to be able to own that scent she wears so well.

Fragranced for Every Season

"Be prepared in season and out of season...." (2 Timothy 4:2)

Seasons are known to be part of divine cycles set forth by God since the beginning when He separated night from day. According to Ecclesiastes 3:1-8,11 there is a time and a season for everything. God has made everything beautiful in its time. Thus, if it is not within God's timing (i.e. when you decide you can do it or you need it right now) the result is rather unattractive.

When God blesses you in its time with whatever it is that has been on your heart, He adds no sorrow with it. (Proverbs 10:22) You don't want to be wearing open-toed sandals during the winter hike with Christ when you should be lacing combat boots. On that same thought, neither do you want to wear the wrong fragrance out of season, repelling a much-needed blessing.

In the book of Ephesians 1:3-14, Paul tells us as believers that because of the work and purpose of Christ achieved at the cross, we have been fragranced for every season. God has thought enough of us to ensure we are fragranced for every season we encounter by allowing us to be beneficiaries of all spiritual blessings in Christ. The day you accepted Christ to be Lord over your life, the kingdom of God in all of its majesty was placed inside of you. The mystery of His will was given to you through every spiritual blessing in God, for every season.

The season of winter is known to us to be cold, arid, and barren. Winter is not the time to sleep, but to be watchful and make provisions for the next season. Those who are not careful will fall into the brittle, deep sleep of idleness. While you are in winter, know that you have already been prepared and equipped to do every good work. Spring is a time of renewal, discovery, and fresh beginnings. When spring blossoms and blankets the earth with the scent of dew, refreshing herself, know you too are being fragranced with restoration, just hold on. Summer is always forecasted with long and laborious days, sweating out curls. Due to the humidity, Satan will try to implant mirages to play tricks on your mind, and whisper in your ear that it's not worth it; you aren't accepted or forgiven. Continue to walk by faith and the spiritual blessing of power in the name of Jesus. We do not wrestle against flesh and blood. Keep in mind, it's not the person, it is the spirit within that person. He has given you power to trample of over all the power of the enemy--so let them run their mouths (they aren't saying anything significant anyway) and you do your thing in the Lord. Do not grow weary in good works, for God has predestined you, giving you a future and a hope. The opinion of others is of no consequence, and of no more importance are their futile efforts to infuse you with fear or regret about why you keep toiling and for what cause, because they don't see fruition. Pray for them, and keep it moving. He didn't give you a spirit of fear, but of love, power, and a sound mind. Girlfriend, don't quit--you have the power within you to endure. Fall is a time to reap the harvest. In the time of autumn, get ready to pop a bottle of the finest sparkling wine and enjoy the fruit of your labor—all smiles.

In Christ, there are seasons within seasons. There will come a season where God is going to stretch your faith, and His work for you at that moment may be so far out of your comfort zone that you'll do a double take and ask God whether He is serious. Remember the spiritual blessing of grace in that season. You have already been predestined and equipped with everything you need—from resources of people to finances, and divine knowledge that you didn't need to go to school for.

What about these spiritual blessings? You can find the intricate details of these upscale and unlimited fragrances in the following passages of scripture: Ephesians 1:3-14, Luke 10:19, Philippians 4:19, and 2 Timothy 1:7. We have been fragranced with being chosen, redeemed, forgiven, loved, adopted, predestined and have inheritance, grace, the Holy Spirit and His will.

We tend to look at what we do not have rather than focusing on what we do have. While we each have been given a measure of faith and our gifts may be different, we all have been given the same amount of every spiritual blessing from the moment we believed. Take a look at the summary below of spiritual blessings we possess as women of God. Consider the dynamic of each one.

Fragranced with Spiritual Blessings

- CHOSEN: called out, separated, children of light
- REDEMPTION: restored; delivered; a debt paid off
- FORGIVENESS: released; cleansed, given mercy, enabled to spiritually breathe
- ADOPTED: accepted, not forsaken, connected to have boldness and access with confidence to Him
- PREDESTINED: prepared beforehand, equipped, strengthened with His might, empowered

- INHERITANCE: eternal life, kingdom and kingdom reign, power, riches of glory
- LOVE: to know the love of Christ which passes knowledge; to be loved without condition
- GRACE: favor, clemency, an entourage of 24/7 bodyguards (angels of the Lord who encamp around you)
- HOLY SPIRIT: to comfort and guide in all truth
- HIS WILL: your purpose within His purpose to partake in His promise

As believers with an every now and again carnal mind, have been deceived to look for the blessings in our lives with natural eyes rather than a spiritual perspective. I want to emphasize that in Christ we have been given everything we will ever need to accomplish the purposes in our lives. Thanks be to God for it, but anything else we get is extra. Understand me. You must not look through natural eyes, but see the spiritual blessings you have. You really don't *need* the house, the car, the man, that purse, or those shoes. Should you happen to need something along the way, He said He would supply all of your needs according to His riches in glory. You have been fragranced (equipped) with every spiritual blessing. You have what the world wants and what it has been searching for in the un-fulfillment and dissatisfaction of people, places, and things. We all want to be forgiven, loved, and accepted. We want grace and the ability to have ready wisdom with the complexities of adult issues, and we have that in the Holy Spirit.

Why do you act in the mentality of a peasant when you have right as a queen and power as a child of God? I'm going to pause right here. I know, I hear some of you essential oils talking: "Well, Jesus came down and made Himself of no reputation." I'll deal with that in a minute. Think about what I just asked you. This is something I need to address further. I have mentioned "kingdom" throughout this book, and it's for good reason--you have one. Do you believe you are a queen and that you have a kingdom? Your perfume is powerful. We have been given the spiritual blessing of inheritance, one being kingdom reign.

Have you ever watched one of those cartoon movies in which the a girl grows up not knowing who she really is, then a turn of events happens at just the right time in order for her to wake up and realize that she has been a queen or princess the entire time? God has given you eyes to see so wake up and smell the perfume. Walk in your anointing. You keep praying to God for this or that, so worried and worn out, but you have it already. You have a kingdom inside of you that cannot be shaken. Everything you need and could ever want is already in your house. (2 Kings 4:1-7)

Now as far as Jesus making Himself of no reputation, He was still all God while He was here. Although He became flesh, He was still omnipotent and omniscient. Like Jesus, it doesn't matter if you are in Heaven or here on Earth, you have been given power, so use it.

When your mindset begins to dwell in the house of the Lord, possessing a kingdom mentality, and fragrancing yourself with the spiritual blessings, you begin to dismiss those natural things you do not have as trivial. You walk a little taller, and with more confidence and poise, as a queen should. When a woman looks good and smells good, people take notice. All you're going see and hear at the astonishment of others is, "What is that perfume you're wearing?"

What happens when we don't fragrance ourselves with spiritual blessings? Confusion, conflict, and competition fill the atmosphere. The content of our divine character collectively as women has been damaged by a few to be exposed by the enemy, and saved or unsaved, we find this entertaining. We sit there and feed ourselves under the spirit of division, but try to fragrance ourselves with unity. What we fail to realize is that Satan is making a laughing spectacle of us. As believers, take off the shades (you look good without them) and open your eyes. God has given you eyes to see. To see what? The lom of God is inside of you. (Luke 17:21) The mystery of His will--and in that, those strategic plans of the enemy meant to bring harm and death to us. We immediately size up and critique how the other is dressed, type of purse carried, car driven, man or no man on arm. If you want the natural blessing, get hold of the spiritual one first. This is what is meant by seeking first the kingdom of God. You have the kingdom already inside of you, but you need to seek out the kingdom. Knowing kingdom principles and order, knowing your right and power, you will know your name.

When your mindset begins to dwell in the house of the Lord, possessing a kingdom mentality, and fragrancing yourself with spiritual blessings, you begin to dismiss those natural things you do not have as trivial. You walk a little taller, and with more confidence and poise, as a queen should. When a woman looks good and smells good, people take notice. All you're going see and hear at the astonishment of others is, "What is that perfume you're wearing?"

It's more than what you can see with your natural eyes. Every time you wear your perfume and spiritual fragrances, you make a choice to live and deepen your relationship with Him. God gave us power of choice and told us in Deuteronomy 30:19 it's highly recommended to choose life and God will love us no matter what choice we decide to make.

I struggled with this principle for the longest time. How can I claim to be a child of God and I'm not this or that? Why am I not highly favored? I have heard my elders speak-- the favor of the Lord ain't fair. Well, my mindset was: "I go to church, I pay my tithes, I'm a good mom, I keep my feet at home, I'm not running the street, I've been saved forever, raised up in the faith, and a laundry list of other Ms. Goody-Two-Shoes stuff, so what is up? Why am I not getting life if I keep doing all this giving?" The key is found in allowing these divine fragrances to *increase* in measure.

"His divine power has given us everything we need for a godly life through our knowledge of Him who called us by His own glory and goodness. Through these, He has given us His very great and precious promises, so that through them you may participate in the divine nature, having escaped the corruption in the world caused by evil desires. For this very reason, make every effort to add to your faith goodness; and to goodness, knowledge; and to knowledge, self-control; and to self-control, perseverance; and to perseverance, godliness; and to godliness, mutual affection; and to mutual affection, love. For if you possess these qualities in increasing measure, they will keep you from being ineffective and unproductive in your knowledge of our Lord Jesus Christ. But whoever does not have them is nearsighted and blind, forgetting that they have been cleansed from their past sins. Therefore, my brothers and sisters,[a] make every effort to confirm your calling and election. For if you do these things, you will never stumble, and you will receive a rich welcome into the eternal kingdom of our Lord and Savior Jesus Christ." (2 Peter 1:3-11).

This is how God uses your fragrances to remember His covenant with you. As you continue increasing in righteousness by using the equipping of these fragrances for every season, taking responsibility for your perfume, you begin to take on the image of Christ, having the mind of Christ. These fragrances fill the nostrils of God, piercing His atmosphere in the throne room as a fragrant aroma, because we are then, at that moment to God, the fragrance of Christ among those who are being saved and among those who are perishing. (2 Corinthians 2:15) When we are about kingdom business, walking in the power of edifying and reminding others of these fragrances as life-leading-to-life, we will not be barren, nor unfruitful. These fragrances remind God of His covenant, His promise that an entrance (a divine gate, or spiritual enlightenment opening) will be supplied to you abundantly into the kingdom when you use the spiritual blessings of what God has given to you to stir up your gift and use it in alignment for the advancement of the kingdom. Give Him a shout of praise!

Perfume and fragrance are intimate gifts. Once engaged in a

bedchamber of fragrance, it resonates in your very core, creating memory and thought, and arousing emotion. We want God to permeate the atmosphere with His presence in our lives--why not saturate His throne room with fragrances given to us in every season we encounter? This is how you make Him remember His covenant with you.

You Can't Smell Your Perfume?

If you can no longer smell your fragrance, it's due to complacency. The Bible calls it a falling away, in Hebrews 6:6. What happens when you become complacent with your perfume? You tend to put more of it on, and it smells like you bathed in it. Yuck! I mean it's just too much at the wrong time. You eventually arrive at the point where you are "holier than thou" and you are no earthly good; you open the door to foolishness, or secretly begin to sleep with the enemy. When you have become accustomed to your scent, it can lead to the monotony of just doing something out of habit. Yes, we sometimes have the audacity to get arrogant with the blessing. Nobody can reprove you or correct you when you are wrong or you get thirsty. When another sister falls, believer or nonbeliever, we may be quick to set judgment with diarrhea of the mouth, gossiping rather than praying, supporting, or edifying one another as we are called to do. All are tendencies of woman who fragrances herself with the black market scent of pride. Sadly, in hopes of retrieving your perfumed scent, it becomes repulsive rather than appealing.

A woman who is fragranced in Christ--knowing who she is in Him, poised in the confidence of Him in her walk and talk—is the epitome of class; she indeed possesses the power to change the atmosphere. It's not her looks that draw you. The attractiveness of the spirit within her sends out a slight breeze of aroma so delicately fragranced that one, if not all, within that room must take notice. The aroma of Christ commands your attention.

Scented for a Purpose

"I must be about My Father's business...." (Luke 2:49)

Perfume, once opened and released, is meant to be used. You are not meant to sit on a shelf and look pretty in your elegantly decorated alabaster box. You are destined to be opened, poured out, and used for the kingdom of God. When you received Jesus into your life and made Him your Lord, salvation did not end at that moment, and your sanctification began. The purpose of perfume and fragrance is that they are meant to be used in service of kingdom business. It is the will of God. We are scented to advance the kingdom for the purpose of bringing life.

His Desire, Your Purpose

In the conversation of restoration and life, your motive and your desire must become His first. If anything you do is not to the glory of God, it is simply done in vain. In Psalm 37:4, it reads: "If you delight yourself in Him, He will give you the desires of your heart." Contrary to popular belief, this scripture does not mean if you delight--as in being nice, acting like a "Christian," or being on your best behavior--that you will get what you want from God. Girl, no! Where does the desire come from? If God didn't give it to you, any work of delighting yourself ("I did this" or "I did that" mentality) is in vain. However, if the desire has come from Him, one that He puts in your heart and not one that you put in your own mind, it has to come to pass. In Matthew 6:33 He says, "Seek ye first the kingdom of God and all 'these things' will be added to you." What are these things? These things are not the car, the house, the husband, or a more than comfortable bank account. Come on, we are talking about God. He is referring to His desires, His plans that will give you hope in your final outcome. Where your treasure is, there your heart will be also. If Jesus is not the center of your heart, who or what is? And if He isn't there taking residence, the restoration you seek will come from man and not God. Those unfulfilled expectations will certainly lead to disappointment. "We shall be satisfied with the goodness of His house," (Psalm 65) so allow God to be your rock and your salvation and not your job, your bestie, or partner.

Let us have this mind in Christ, in which His desire which will become our desires. Could it be the reason why you are overworking yourself so hard, being so busy (and not productive) in the church or whatever while at the same time stressing yourself out, is because the desire is your own, and not His? As a believer, when your desires do not become one with His, it profits nothing, and all is done in vain. When your desire becomes His desire, serving Him won't seem like a chore. When you delight yourself in Him, the Bible becomes more than a book. As His word gets rooted in you, it is life even in the most detestable circumstances. When His desires become yours, all the resources needed are readily at your disposal. You have read in the previous chapter that you are fragranced with every spiritual blessing. Everything else is extra. Hence, it gives more meaning to Philippians

4:17: "And my God will supply all of your needs according to His riches in glory."

Endurance will not become a task, like something you have to check off your list. When your desires become His desires it is at this time we engage in the life, and life more abundantly. This is not to say we will not go through the furnace of affliction, but that's when we see that furnace of affliction as a light one, which gains for us a more eternal weight of glory. (2 Corinthians 4:17) That's when our eyes are opened and we can count it all joy when we fall into various trials and mean it.

If faith comes by hearing and hearing by the word of God, hear this: You can delight yourself in Him only when the desires in your heart are not your own. His desires derive from and are "kingdom business." He says in His word, the kingdom of God is inside of you. (Luke 17:21) Your purpose is divine. You are created to do fabulously great and amazing things.

Scented to Bring Life

In 2 Corinthians 2:15 the Word tells us that to some we are the smell of death and to others, the fragrance of life. We are influential regardless of the aroma we present entering or exiting a room. As a Perfumed Letter, we are the fragrance of life to all we encounter. We will get to a more definitive explanation of what a Perfumed Letter is within the next few chapters. Yes, it is true that Christians are sub-consciously put to a higher standard known and read by all men. An unbeliever will recognize the very second when they see or hear something foul in a Christian by capitalizing their judgment on what is and is not Christ-*like*.

We are scented for the purpose of bringing life, not only to the perishing, but that our own descendants may live. The Bible speaks in Genesis 28 to choose life so that you and your descendants may live. What we do today is certain to affect our tomorrow. Are the choices you are making today bringing life or death to the greatest of your grandchildren? Oh, if you realized what power you have been given! Physically and spiritually, you have the power to give birth and liberation to nations with just one seed. Will the generational curse cease with you, or continue down the line? When we choose life, the perfume poured out from within us resonates with our descendants. You have to pour out in order to be filled and to overflow. When we choose life, it is more than making the right decision, it is a godly one. The words you speak about yourself and those who come from your natural womb and spirit carry a tremendous amount of weight. (Proverbs 18:21) None of the influences of friends, school, and media have the same colossal power found within you.

Accountability

Can we blame God for the state the world is in? God gave us this planet to reign over and rule, and the choice is ours whether or not we want Him in our lives. In losing sight of our purpose, we have become desensitized to the spiritual war right before us. This explains the unnecessary struggle that keeps breeding generational curses and incubating death. It is because we have not made the decision to choose life so that our descendants may live. Flow with me. I am speaking spiritually as well. The seeds of gifts and talents that God has given you bring Him glory and life to others when you choose to stir them up. (1Timothy 4:14-16) Ladies, you have such power from on high--I need you to get off your behind and get on your purpose for being here. In the beginning of this book, I told you that we are not here for ourselves. We are here to help others by bringing life and restoration, especially those who have yet to believe. Only what you do for Christ will last. He is life, and when you choose life, someone else gets the blessing to live.

A benefit of being scented for a purpose is that your perfume is His purpose. There was a woman who poured out her perfume to Jesus and the aroma filled the entire house. (John 12:1-8) Many thought she was crazy and stupid for having done so, but she made Jesus remember her, by saturating His atmosphere, and thus she will be remembered forever. She recognized what her fragrance was; she used it to pour out to Jesus and it filled the house. The Word tells us that a wise woman builds her house and on the other hand, a foolish woman tears her house down. (Proverbs 14:1) When you tear your house down, your descendants—spiritual and natural--will have no-where to lay their heads. If one cannot lie down, one will not be able to relax and sleep in peace; therefore, because you did not fill your house with your perfume, nations of generations and dynasties suffer and struggle. This is not about you. One house has the potential to become a nation, and a nation a generation, and a generation a dy-nasty. In a house are rooms, and the Bible says rooms are filled with special treasures. This treasure is in earthen vessels. (2 Corinthinas 4:7) Your children need the house to be filled with your perfume and fragrances so that even while they are sleeping in their rooms, they may be filled and blessed. Be careful whom you fill a house with, for there may be some who are strongly opposed, as well as those who will ridicule and not see the blessing and favor of your having done so. To use perfume to fill the wrong house, one in which Jesus does not reside, will cause you to put in all the work of on-the-job-training into a man and have him not bless you with a ring and the com-mitment of marriage. Not using or abusing your perfume to fill your house breeds generational curses, wounds nations, and dismantles dynasties that would otherwise have thrived in their inheritance and early kingdom advancement. Sadly, you can see many examples of this and some perfumes released rightly in the books of 2 Kings and 2 Chronicles for further study. It is important to note that throughout these books, mention is made by name of the women, the mothers of young men who chose not to fill their house with perfume, and the grave consequences.

You are raising children--whether or not they were birthed through your natural or spiritual womb--to be fit for the kingdom of God. You are raising purpose. You are instilling principle. When was the last time you "charged" your child or gift? Turn to 1 Kings 2:2-4 and take mental note of how David did it. Paraphrasing this passage of scripture, David charged Solomon with walking in the ways of the Lord and specifically told him to do so that the Lord may keep His promise to David. God promised David that if his descendants would watch how they lived, and would serve the Lord with all their heart and soul, David's kingdom would forever reign. Wow, that's powerful! You mean to tell me, if you choose life, God will keep His promise for generation after generation, given the little ones act right? The catch is that in order for them to act right, they need to see *you* living right. Even if they do wrong, God keeps His promise. (2 Chronicles 21, Proverbs 22:6)

Reflection: God has appointed a set time for your perfume to be released, and when it is released it should bring the aroma of life to those whom you encounter. There is no greater love than for a man to lay down his life for his friends. (John 15:13) Scented for the purpose of restoration, that's exactly what you do. When you choose life, you lay down your life for another. There will be certain things you cannot do and words you cannot speak. Royalty can't just act any old kind of way. When you restore and bring life, you break generational curses and release liberation of other kingdoms and nations. This happens when you give and you have nothing left to give, when you pray for others yet you are standing in need of prayer, and when you love past the pain and pressing despite the hurt, abuse, and betrayal. Laying down your life for His people and doing it to the least of them, you have done it unto God, as life leading to life so that others may live.

The Real Cost of Your Perfume—His and Hers

"You were bought with a price...." (1 Corinthians 7:23)

According the Guinness Book of World Records, the most expensive perfume is the Clive Christian No.1 for Men or No.1 for Women - 30 ml (1 fl oz) of which typically costs $1,317 (then $2,355). In November 2005, Clive Christian created No.1 Imperial Majesty, a ten-bottle, limited edition of the Clive Christian No 1 Collection, priced at $115,000 (then $205,000) per 500 ml (17 fl oz). The perfume was presented in a Baccarat crystal flacon, decorated with a five-carat white diamond and an 18-carat gold collar. It was launched at the Roja Dove Haute Parfumerie in Harrods, London, UK and sold over Christmas both there and at Bergdorf Goodman in New York, USA. The price included delivery in a Bentley.

Girl, I was shaking my head too when I read those facts the first time. I have a question for you. If a natural manmade perfume costs over $205,000, how much more is yours worth? When you begin to walk in the understanding of what you are worth and the value of your perfume, people will treat you accordingly, and your enemies will take notice.

What makes a perfume expensive? Is it the brand name alone, the packaging, the ingredients? Together, all play a part in the perfume's expense. However, what makes a perfume valued and prized are the pure concentration of the rarity of the oil comprised within it. You cannot put a price on it, and even to touch it or come within the experience of the scent, one has to be favored. Your perfume is unique and priceless, substance combination of two parts--His and hers.

His

The first substance is the oil of Jesus Christ Himself, The Anointed One. In case you need a reminder about why your perfume costs so much and why you can't just do what you want to do as a believer, and why we have to be living sacrifices as so forth, take a look at the following list. Jesus...

- was not defined as eye candy as being beautiful in appearance to be desired
- was an outcast, hated by all
- was rejected and cut off from society
- was sick with sorrow
- was so unattractive, people hid their faces from Him
- carried every burden of every sin past, present, and future
- was wrongly accused and wounded for our wrongdoings
- was obedient to the cross
- was bruised by the Lord but bruised for our iniquities
- was chastised for our peace
- was beaten by man, afflicted by God
- was oppressed because of us
- poured out His soul asking if this fate could be removed from

Him, but within the same thought pressed on and said Thy will be done
- was offered for sin in our place
- carried your cross
- was spit upon
- had nails hammered in the center of both hands and feet
- in spite of such unimaginable, excruciating pain, still had enough love to intercede on behalf of His abusers and ask God for their forgiveness

The main key ingredient that makes your perfume "priced far above rubies" is the amount of concentrated, pure oil within--and that's Jesus. Another pricey ingredient is wisdom. The Bible says although it costs you all you have, get understanding. (Proverbs 4:7) Commonality is *not* in your fragrance wardrobe. You are mistaken if you believe the price of wisdom will ever be marked down. His oil set you apart at a price, and you are to act accordingly.

Hers

Jesus is one part of the substance combination, and you are the other, passionately known as "hers." It cost Jesus His life, and the Bible tells us as He is, so are we in this world. Read the passage of scripture found in Isaiah 61:1-10.

In the very first verse, it clearly states you are anointed (perfumed) and goes on to say that:

- you have power to heal the brokenhearted
- you can proclaim liberty to captives
- you can proclaim the year and day of the Lord and his vengeance (go take your blessing, God said it's yours)
- you can comfort and console

- you can help give another sister beauty for her ashes and joy
- you have a garment of praise to help encourage and edify when one feels heavy

What these passages collectively mention is the pressing of your life's petals—the ciphering of your oil for the benefit of others, that God may be glorified. 2 Corinthians 4: 8 NKJV reads:

"We are hard pressed on every side, yet not crushed; we are perplexed, but not in despair; persecuted, but not forsaken; struck down, but not destroyed— always carrying about in the body the dying of the Lord Jesus, that the life of Jesus also may be manifested in our body. For we who live are always delivered to death for Jesus' sake, that the life of Jesus also maybe manifested in our mortal flesh."

That is what meant by taking up your cross.

Perfume in itself is already influential. Your perfume rebuilds and repairs cities and generations. These cities are your neighborhoods and the ministries you have as a mother, wife, sister, and friend. When you wear your perfume, your anointing is liberating--so much so that generations that come forth from your womb are blessed. God makes good on His promise and you receive the double honor and double possession for the pressing. A widow in the Bible realized the important cost of pouring out the oil within her in 2 Kings 4:1-7.

Don't get it twisted; I'm not here to feed you a story about prosperity and how pretty you look. You already know that you have it going on and if you are in Christ, you know you are fragranced with every spiritual blessing. You have more than enough. Your perfume smells so extraordinary; He made it so no one can rock it better than you. You get the tangible when the intangible is taken care of, and it is worth more than you can imagine. The anointing you have is superior grade. It is of high quality, and quality costs. What has it cost you? Please take a good look at your ingredients from the pressings endured in your own life that have brought about a scent so lovely, and divinely made for you.

Your Worth in Christ

I have heard many times with a subliminal undertone: "You are expensive," as in "not worth it." After hearing that so many times from the enemy puppeting certain people, I started to believe the lie, that maybe they are right, I'm not worth the cost considering my past and present state, so I had let myself go in the spirit and stopped taking care of myself by the Word. I didn't bother fighting the enemy because I became one myself, believing them rather than what Jesus had to say about my worth. I believed a lie because I didn't know the truth, the real cost of my perfume. The enemy knew who I was, and I did not. With the true value you hold as a Daughter of the Most High God, not everyone can afford your worth--and honey, that is their problem, not yours. No matter if your employer refuses acknowledge your worth on payroll, or even your father didn't recognize you as a little girl growing up how special and valued you were, or how a parent favored other siblings over you. Either way, we have been blinded in regard to our worth and when this happens, the enemy eats it up and in turn we devalue our own perfume. Let me intercede with a word to the wise: whatever perfume or cologne you are yoked up with, seek the origin of its spirit. If his or her spirit is not in line with His, say goodbye. The anointing you have and the kingdom that is inside of you have eternal worth, so treat yourself as such. To appreciate, honor, and respect your perfume (your anointing) that spirit must meet or exceed yours in its own value, so watch out for wolves in sheep' clothing, and "guard your heart, for out it spring the issues of life." (Proverbs 4:23)

Not Being Mean, But I'm a Realist

I am confident of this one thing...it will cost to dwell in the house of the Lord forever. Nothing worth having is microwaved. It is usually marinated, baked, broiled, boiled, grilled, or slow-cooked in a Crock-Pot. It will cost you to stand up for what you believe in, and to fail in order to succeed. It may cost a friend, a fast, intercessory prayer, and love, a substantial investment of time, money, maturity level, and tears. How many tears have you cried at night? I mean the hot tears that run like the Nile, or those tears you cry because you know you're a Christian and can't do anything about it in flesh. From the hours given and spent in dedication to make that dream come to a reality, to applying mind renewal every day (Romans 12:2) and patience (James 2:2-4)--quality costs.

There's something about the cost of our perfume. Think about it, ladies. What is it that we possess that Satan wants so badly? Why is he after us with such great motivation? It's more than your liquid sunshine, okay, and your pretty face. Why would he desire to destroy your life so? Why does he want to steal any peace or joy you may have and kill the dreams you had as a little girl? Could it be that we have the power from our perfume to bring forth and influence life? Could it be that the kingdom within has the power to bring life to dynasties? "We have this treasure in earthen vessels that the excellence of the power of God may be of God and not of us." (2 Corinthians 4:7, NKJV) Let the enemy come, because yes ma'am, you are a strong woman indeed; "for strong is the One who executes His Word." (Joel 2:11) Be encouraged. 2 Corinthians 4:16-18, NKJV reads: "Therefore we do not lose heart. Even though our outward man is perishing, yet the inward man is being renewed day by day. For our light affliction, which is but for a moment, is working for us a far more exceeding and eternal weight of glory, while we do not look at the things which are seen, but at the things which are not seen. For the things which are seen are temporary, but the things which are not seen are eternal." It's going to be okay.

Your perfume was fixed and bought at a price. It does not go on sale, will never go on the clearance rack, and its value is unimaginable. God has fragranced you and a given you a perfume all your own to be a blessing to another. No, you cannot do what everybody else is doing. You are called out as the elect of God. It may cost, but the aroma of life-leading-to-life that you bring is worth it, so the cost is necessary.

The Roman historian Pliny wrote, "The very highest recommendation of them is, that when a female passes by, the odor which proceeds from her may possibly attract the attention of those even who till then are intent upon something else. In price they exceed so large a sum […] so vast is the amount that is paid for a luxury made not for our own enjoyment, but for that of others; for the person who carries the perfume about him is not the one, after all, that smells it."

Declaration

The next time you come across a spirit (not literally a person or situation, see Ephesians 6:12) who is ignorant of your worth, remind yourself and them: "You're right, I am expensive. I am worth the expense. You have no idea how much the essence of me really costs, you cannot put a price on my perfume. The cross I bear is not a simple object. It's not separate from me, it *is* me. It is life. It costs me to wear, but it cost my Lord and Savior Jesus His life, so I owe it to Him to give Him mine. My Father is the King of Kings and Lord of Lords. Do you know who your daddy is? I am my Father's daughter, a daughter of the Most High God. My Dad is called I AM. I am of a royal priesthood and have right and power. Under my Daddy's name, I can decree and declare a thing--speaking it into existence and it is so. My Father provides me with an entourage of 24/7 security because the angels of the Lord encamp all around me. Yes, I am expensive. I am a citizen of heaven. I come from premium-top-grade luxury that man cannot fathom, nor has the materials to manufacter. You should count it a privilege that He allowed my aroma to be briefly released in your atmosphere. I make my boast in the Lord! Do not confuse this with arrogance, for I am confident in the Lord."

So the next time a spirit addresses you as "expensive" in a tone that is derogatory, devaluing you in any way, you remind it of who you are and whose you are. You come at a price, and you are worth it. All this pain you have gone through, the piercing and puncture in places that have leaked oil. All the crap endured, tears shed carrying around a shield of faith when you are exhausted; the bruises, broken stems, and crushed petals pressed once more, aid in the sum total cost of your perfume.

Reflection: Due to its rare ingredients and laborious processing, your perfume is a highly sought-after commodity. What has your perfume cost you? More importantly, do you realize that one slight breeze of your scent transcends this earthly realm? It's okay if they can't afford the friendship or relationship; don't take it personally. Not everyone can pay full price for quality. The friendship or relationship was souring your perfume anyway, so the Lord arranged and allowed certain things to take place for your good. Do not despise the cost- -though it cost you all you have, understand it, and embrace your worth.

Perfumed Letters

"Written in our hearts...written not with ink, but with the Spirit of the Living God." (2 Corinthians 3: 2-3)

What Is a Perfumed Letter?

We know letters are a form of communication between the sender and receiver. A Perfumed Letter is a woman who has boldly confessed with her mouth and believed within in her heart that God raised Jesus from the dead. She is a certified true testimony that Jesus lives. She has come into the understanding that she is an original, hand-scribed letter written with the ink of His Spirit and sealed by the Holy Spirit. She is the righteousness of God; not by feeling or opinion, but fact, because when (paraphrased) *"He made Him who knew no sin to be sin for her, she became the righteous of God in Him."* (2 Corinthians 5:21) When a Perfumed Letter walks by, people take notice, and it's not because of her fashion style. The gentle breeze that precedes her incorruptible beauty entry and exit to a room of a gentle and quiet spirit (1 Peter 3:4) leaves an indelible impression. A Perfumed Letter's way pleases the Lord so that even her enemies are at peace with her. She may not be on her game one weekend and have a bad girl moment in the cool of the day, but that does not take away her righteousness. Society does not have to forgive her and present her with a sticker, for she has been forgiven by The One who matters most. Perfumed Letters are relational, not religious. She knows she is a woman fragranced with every spiritual blessing and created within the inscription of His likeness, yet showered by His signature fragrance, Love. She is the aroma of life-leading-to-life as the fragrance of Christ.

We know that God has given each of us a very fine perfume at a great price, complete with fragrances to aid in supporting such an extraordinary scent. In grasping this truth in the study of previous chapters, we now understand the process and purpose in the privilege of being a Perfumed Letter. Walking in spiritual wisdom of fragrancing yourself with perfume, we know this is a profoundly intimate and personal relationship with our Lord. It transforms our perspective, externally and internally, while simultaneously seeping into the pores, for she knows Him as Eve knew Adam, becoming one with His spirit, worshipping Him in spirit and in truth.

You Should Know

You are an original, a hand-scribed letter, God-scented with the aroma of Christ. Written inside of you, you are a walking inscription of Him, of His likeness in spirit and in truth. You are the fragrance that fills the nostrils of God every time you pray, worship, or praise, and walk in spiritual blessing. You are a Perfumed Letter written in our hearts, known and read by all men. You were here in His Spirit when He made the heavens and the earth. "God has anointed us and set His seal of ownership on us, and put His Spirit in our hearts." (2

Corinthians 1:21, 22) He is the only answer to quench the thirst your soul longs for. No matter how independent you may be or how far you distance yourself from Him, even if it's on purpose, the perfume, the anointing inside of you, and His love that pierces the inmost corners of your soul cannot be filled with people or material possessions.

The Message of a Perfumed Letter

Remember the old-fashioned romantic letters written in cursive? Well, those special letters took time to write, and it added a personal touch for both the sender and receiver when the letter was fragranced with perfume. To enjoy the message, no matter how long or short, the letter was composed of three main parts: greeting, body, and a closing. From a spiritual aspect, the greeting of a Perfumed Letter is remembrance, the body is the testament, and the closing is the influence. Finally, the Perfumed Letter is fragranced and always sealed with "love" by the Holy Spirit. Overall, the message, context, or vibe of the letter could is the aromatic scent of life for the recipient.

Remembrance

The first intent of a Perfumed Letter is the greeting of remembrance. Scent evokes memory, and the written word makes it official. This is twofold. On one hand, we are to help others by reminding them, jogging their memory of who they were before the fall. We are to remind others of the significance of Christ's work at the cross, His promise of redemption. Redemption of mankind is the reason why Jesus came from His throne to earth. Redemption brings about reconciliation. When the world sees you, they should be automatically reminded or their originality in Christ. Two, when you recognize the privilege of being a Perfumed Letter, each time that you pray or wear the spiritual blessings, you fill the nostrils of God with your fragrance and He remembers his covenant with you.

Testament

A Perfumed Letter is a certified true living testimony of God. The old self has passed away and all have become new. In Hebrews 9:16-17, NIV it reads: "In the case of a will [testament], it is necessary to prove the death of the one who made it, because a will is in force only when somebody has died; it never takes effect while the one who made it is living. It reigns true today. A will is only effective after the testator dies. Then and only then will property, monies, and the like be divided among beneficiaries." Spiritually, we are to die daily to the flesh and each time that we walk in our deliverance and redemption; it becomes a testament to others that Jesus lives.

Back in the day, in the old church, we used to have testimony service. This was a designated period in the program in which anyone was free to stand up and testify about what miracles, deliverance, blessings, and favor the Lord had done in their lives. It reinforced the good news of the gospel and the power of His resurrection. It brought home encouragement and truth: "If Jesus did that for them, I know He can do it for me too."

While many contemporary, modern churches have withdrawn the element of testimony service from their programs, as a Perfumed Letter it is the embodiment of our character as to why we are the way we are. We are a testimony. Testimony is the underlying motive driving our perfume and fragrance as dead to sin and alive to Christ, that "miracle-working power."

The world has a mentality of see-it-to-believe-it. From the girls and guys you used to roll deep with, to exes who could very well get you to speak in other tongues, to those days and nights of situations and behaviors trying to find yourself or fulfill yourself behind closed doors and under sheets that you ended up wishing never happened. You're not perfect, but you certainly don't smell like the black market scents of yesterday. I'm not saying go tell your business details out loud to everyone you meet. The Holy Spirit will let you know when the opportunity has presented itself, for He will give you what to speak in that hour. What better way to share Jesus to a blind and dying world than your testament of what you have gone through, how God delivered and set you free to be an encouragement to another? Most of the time, you may not have to verbally speak anything, because as a Perfumed Letter, as you continue to walk in the Spirit, the world will read it anyway and know. Your background may not be a pretty picture, but your testimonies are righteous and faithful, good for meditation. (Psalm 119: 138, 99)

Perfumed Letters, as understood in a previous chapter, the magnitude of our influence is incalculable, ranging from natural generations to spiritual kingdoms. We are known and read by the world as our lifestyles fill the body of each letter. Those words, actions, and thoughts must be infused with His oil so that when we are read by all men, they are reading the word and seeing truth. The Word of God says in 2 Corinthians 2:14 NIV, "God uses us to spread the aroma of the knowledge of Him everywhere." In Philippians 4:5 we are told to "let our gentleness be known to all" (and that's gentleness without a roll of the eyes or a twist of the neck). What will they read? Are they being imparted with knowledge, or imagination? Will they read a love letter filled with compassion and mercy, or one of judgment?

Truth

When we hear truth, there is no room to turn back to ignorance. Saved or not, we are held accountable by truth. If you don't wear sunscreen, you could get burned. Should you not rinse the relaxer out in time; your scalp will have some irritation. Choose not to wrap it up; there is a strong possibly of pregnancy or a sexually transmitted disease. If you have no control over your spirit, you are like a city broken down without walls where anything or anyone can come in and have reign in your life. After hearing the truth, it is a matter of choice beyond that as to what we do with it. The Bible says in Ephesians

1:13, NIV: "And you were also included in Christ when you heard the word of truth, the gospel of your salvation. Having believed, you were marked in Him with a seal, the promised Holy Spirit." And that seal was a "Love Always." 2 Timothy 2:19, NKJV puts it this way: "Nevertheless, the solid foundation of God stands, having this seal: The Lord knows those who are His and Let everyone who names the name of Christ depart from iniquity." At the time when you hear the truth but harden your heart and don't act right, He will chastise you—but only because He loves you.

Sealed with Love

Perfumed Letters, we mist, spray, and dab on signature fragrances of Christ daily to build up ourselves and others in encouragement, courage, inspiration, and hope to bring life. From the ex who can't seem to get himself together but yet told you that you didn't act right and to get a life, to the father who was absentee by neglect yet lived within driving distance, to those females who you thought had your back but who acted instead in betrayal, telling all your business but theirs—despite all, a lady keeps herself rightly perfumed. How does she do that? Wisdom of Application. A wise woman builds her house, while the foolish tears it down with her hands and though it costs all she has, she gets understanding, knowing His divine order, her position and place.

We both know you are an attractive woman, but what perfume or fragrance are you wearing that causes people to be drawn to or repelled from Christ? Everyone is drawn to love. We cannot function without it. People may be attracted to your appearance, but it is your scent that draws them in and the words in your letter that keep them captivated. From woman to woman, I ask, what are they really reading about you, versus what God wants them to see? Are they able to see Christ through your letter? Go with me to 2 Chronicles 20:1-30. I know Jehoshaphat is a guy, but bear with me in the spirit, because the message is the same.

Jehoshaphat had people coming to tell him bad news that added to the drama of things already "against" him in his life. The news came at a bad time. He was already being pressed on other matters. Can you see Christ in his letter?

1) Direct to God. He went immediately went to the Lord for help--not his significant other, not a bestie, nor a mom-knows-best type deal. He went directly to the Lord. What is inside of you will come out, and obviously he knew what to do and who to go to for help.

2) Prayer and Remembrance. He addressed the problem quickly in prayer. He didn't have time to cry or get depressed. He reminded God of who He was, and His power. He reminded God of past breakthroughs.

3) Confidence. He believed in the power of prayer and had confidence that God heard his prayer.

4) Humility. He understood he could not get through this alone and unashamedly but boldly came to the throne and told God, "I don't know what to do." By doing this, he opened the door for God to have full reign.

After the prayer, God indeed answered, but He answered through another individual. Expect God to answer but forget the details of how, where, and whom He will answer through. Honestly, you probably don't want to know the truth in that. I have to make mention here, as believers it is imperative to be able to hear that still voice. As you grow in your walk with God, by the time you have crossed from concrete to absolute, you will learn, if you have not learned already how to distinguish between your voice, His, and Satan's. It's going to take more than a few trips to the Garden for extensive pressing to figure it out.

How would you know the difference? Simple. If you are walking in the Spirit, you will not fulfill the lusts of the flesh; this means that anything having to do with the lust of the eyes, the lust of the flesh, and the pride of life (1 John 2:16) will not be a hindrance blocking His voice. Two, having the Holy Spirit within you, you have a ready comforter who will lead you and guide you in all truth. Not some, not only spiritual truths, but ALL truth.

Now back to the message. We know that God answered the prayer, but He gave instructions--also known as the preservatives--on how to obtain the blessing.

Preservation in Instruction

When faced with the pressing, a Perfumed Letter should generally read like this from 2 Chronicles 1-30:

1) Fear not. God told Jehoshaphat, "Do not be afraid or discouraged for the battle is not yours, but God's."

2) Confrontation. Confront the principality, not the person. Get up in the enemy's face (spiritually speaking). Remember, we wrestle not against flesh and blood. (Ephesians 6:12) Think about what you have going on in your life right now. It is not that person or situation that is the problem; it's the spirit, the principality within it that's the issue. This is not the time to be cute, or to be shy with words. Under the authority of the blood of Jesus, remind the devil and his boys who you are, whose you are, and that you will not tolerate foolishness or babysit his crap.

3) Go in stealth. God openly told and exposed the enemy's location. Nope, that was not grimy. As a believer, you have been given eyes to see and eyes to hear via spiritual wisdom. He will provide a way of escape for you, but you have to know His voice.

4) Courtesy reminder. God reminded him you don't have

to fight--take your position, stand firm, and see your deliverance.

5) Again, fear not. God knows human thought quite well; He repeated Himself to him: Do not be afraid or discouraged. When you are scared, when you feel like you can't and snail up in fear, rather than walking by faith—remember not to be afraid. Because God is for you, who can be against you? Do it scared.

6) Go out and face your enemy. God is confrontational. He prepares a table before you *in* the presence of your enemies (Psalm 23:5) intentionally pampering you in front of their rolling eyes. They may be laughing now and think they have a heads up on you, because they had front row seats to your past, but lady, keep your cool. It gives God great pleasure to trouble those who trouble you. (2 Thessalonians 1:6)

7) Worship Him. After Jehoshaphat received his answered prayer, he worshipped the Lord.

8) Praise Him. While you have ushered in His presence by worship, praise Him thereafter. The praise that is going up to the Lord is used to set ambushes against your enemy and defeat them.

9) Heed to His voice. Jehosphat went where God told him. God wants your obedience even after the victory. Will you still be able to hear Him after you have been delivered, or will you go back and do your own thing till you need Him again?

10) Taste the goodness of Lord. Enjoy your fruit. The Bible states that Jehoshaphat's blessing was more than what he could take away.

In Verse 29, Jehoshaphat was being watched (read by all men) seeing how God received the glory of testimony. The Word tells us that in that hour, "the fear of God came upon all the kingdoms... when they heard how the Lord fought against the enemies of Israel." The world may not have seen you pray, but it's the Perfumed Letter that has told them plenty. They need to be reminded in memory of who they are and can be in Christ, and see the testament in your life-style that God is real and His love is unconditional.

Reflection: God has taken the time to intricately and intimately write a personal letter, touched with perfume, for the world to read. It gives "message in a bottle" a whole new meaning. You are a Perfumed Letter, written not with ink, but the Spirit of the Living God. It is a privilege to be written with perfumed words that cannot be erased and will not fade. What does that mean to you? Transparency? Honor? Does it mean to eliminate excuses and walk in the Spirit? Do the words in your letter jump out with open arms, revealing unconditional love to ignite change and kindle compassion toward those who don't look like you? Do your letters bring life? You are an epistle of Christ, written by the Spirit of the living God--what are they reading about you?

Exclusive Fragrance Reviews

Listed in Alphabetical Order

Drama Queen

Review: Disgraceful. Theatrical top notes release trouble, an out-of-control zest, gossip and whispers that separate the closest of friends. Composed with foul heart notes of exaggerated emotional pageantry and diversion, Drama Queen is driven by the base note of a long-standing attention deficit. Caution: Drama Queen is a sultry manipulation also supported by an extreme base of emptiness. There is no rest for the wearer who fragrances herself with this. (Isaiah 57:20-21)

Perfumista(s): Herodias (Mark 6), Woman of Tekoa (2 Samuel 14:1-20), Queen Jezebel (1 Kings 18, 21, 2 Kings 9), Queen Athalia (2 Chronicles 22), Rebekah (Genesis 27), Delilah (Judges 16)

Envy

Review: Dangerously spicy. A rancid, intense scent for all women. It preludes bitterness and hatred. Harbored by dominant blends of idleness, regret and selfishness create the background for this fragrance. Caution: Avoid this scent by being content in every state you are in minding your own business, and working with your own hands (1 Thessalonians 4:11) pressing forward.

Perfumista(s): Miriam (Miriam (Numbers 12:1-15), Peninnah (1Samuel 1), Rachel (Genesis 29, 30), Lot's Wife (Genesis 19)

Fierce Faith

Review: This fragrance is not for those who faint in the day of adversity. Fierce Faith is a courageous, strengthening fragrant aroma that poses as a stimulant for the wearer to be hood fight, battle-ready, and inextinguishable. Although it presents an evocative blend of notes-- perseverance, character, and hope--the base of the fragrance is supported by your belief in God that this too (whatever is being asked, sought, or knocked upon) will pass. Fine print: Fierce Faith will stretch you beyond your comfort zone, but carries a sure reward.

Perfumista (s): Woman with Blood Issue (Luke 8), Jochebed (Moses' mother, Exodus 1) Rahab (Hebrews 11:31, Joshua 2, 6), Jael (Judges 4)

Forgiveness

Review: Forgiveness is one of those on-the-go fragrances as we may never know when we may need to mist it here or there. It has de-stress notes of compassion and mercy, but the base for this aroma is love. A release of power happens within you when this fragrance is applied to yourself and others, breaking rusty chains of captivity or grudges, and welcoming liberation. Keep a mini spray bottle in your purse.

Perfumista(s): Woman at the Well (John 8)

Fragrance of Prayer

Review: A must-have! As one of top-selling fragrances of all time, it is a fragrance you cannot leave home without. This scent is delicate, but not to be underestimated. It carries strong reverential top and bottom notes toward Jesus and God our Father. The heart note of faith is the key to this fragrance. While the heart notes of faith are the substance of things hoped for and the evidence of things not seen, this aroma has such power that it can fill the nostrils of God, create a more intimate relationship between you and the Lord, open windows of heaven, grant protection, blessings of open and shut doors, literally out-of-this-world miracles, and so much more! Try it once and you'll be hooked. You will be astonished at what one ounce of it in your life can do.

Perfumista(s): Esther (Book of Esther), Hannah (1 Samuel 1), Hagar (Genesis 16 & 21)

Fruit Smoothie

Review: The Fruit Smoothie is a wonderful blend that should be in every woman's fragrance wardrobe. While the base note is love, this fruity melody has top and middle notes of joy, peace, longsuffering, kindness, goodness, faithfulness, gentleness, and self-control.

Perfumista: (Your name)

Humility

Review: An unappealing fragrance by world standard of pride, but a beautiful invitation to honor. Humility is denial of self. It's a woman-up and close your mouth scent. It presents a modest regard for one's own state by placing concern and or praise for others rather than yourself. It releases a strengthening grace of God for the wearer.

Perfumista(s): Deborah (Judges 4 & 5), the widow (Mark 12:41-44)

Infrared

Review: Caution. It's okay to be angry, but do not let your anger linger. Read the fine print on the warning label found in Ephesians 4:26, NIV: "In your anger do not sin: Do not let the sun go down while you are still angry." The top carries a cold numbness. At the core, the wearer experiences a heart note of feverish foul hatred that is virtually nonexistent of love. What gives this fragrance its zeal is the base note of black bitterness at the root. This fragrance can cause internal damage spiritually and physically; it can emasculate the human psyche of the wearer and others absorbed by this scent.

Perfumista(s): Queen Athaliah (2 Kings 11, 2 Chronicles 22 & 23), Queen Jezebel (1 Kings 15, 19, 21 & 2 Kings 9), Herodias (Mark 6)

Joy

Review: Absolutely invigorating. A vibrant blend of laughter and merry "heart" notes. The strength of this fragrance is known to diffuse itself late in the midnight hour and later comes full circle in the morning with citrus bursts of unspeakable joy.

Perfumista(s): Elizabeth (Luke 1), Sarah (Genesis 18, 21)

Love

Review: Eternal. Love has blossoming soft, subtle, and uplifting top notes that make it a highly sought-after, long-standing classic for any collection. Transcending heart notes are composed of strength, authenticity, and richly unconditional essences. The base for this beautiful scent is the pure concentration depth of God, for God is love. When Love is released into the atmosphere, unexplained changes can occur for the better. As it fragrances the chambers of the heart with kindness and goodness, it harnesses the power to cover all offenses and ascend beyond death. It is majestically breathtaking. Love can also be discovered individually in sets of: Agape, Eros, Philia, and Storge.

Perfumista(s): Shunammite Woman (2 Kings 4), Rizpah (2 Samuel 21)

Pretty Pretender
Review: Beginning top notes are flirty, but carry dark motives. The heart notes are a smooth blend of 100% chameleon deception. Spontaneous flashes of mischief gleam in the heart of this scent, leaving the one who fragrances herself with it oblivious that her conscience is seared. Warning: This fragrance is an abomination to the Lord and will cause the wearer to forsake mercy. (Jonah 2:8)

Perfumista(s): Wife of Jeroboam (1 Kings 14:1-17), Woman of Tekoa (2 Samuel 14:1-20)

Pride
Review: Stank in a bottle. Beginning with notes of arrogance and repulsiveness, Pride is an irresistible fragrance to many. The heart of Pride is ego and conceit. Wearers often release "I can do no wrong" attitudes and "Don't need any help" mentalities. Base note: all-about-me. Its aftereffect is shame that is guaranteed after a hard fall.

Perfumista(s): Sapphira (Acts 5), Gomer (Hosea)

Restoration
Review: Topped with grace and mercy impressions, Restoration has a sheer sweetness to it. It has influences of a peppermint wake-up to stay on the narrow path. The heart notes are a creation of gratefulness and servitude. The base notes overflow with a bouquet of compassion and forgiveness. Restoration is the perfect gift for any occasion.

Pefumista (s): Dorcas (Acts 9), Slave girl (Acts 16), Mary of Bethany (John 12, Mark 14), Gomer (Hosea)

Scent of Brokenness

Review: Soft and tender to touch, this scent provokes the wearer to be pliable with the ability to be shaped and transformed in hands of God. Top notes ring with a fragile searing pain. While the pain fades, heart notes engulf the experience with a cooling comfort of the Holy Spirit and God's love. Warning label directly states: This fragrance is painful to the core of your being, but a broken and contrite heart God does not despise. Contrary to popular belief, this scent ensures that the wearer is in the best place to be with closing notes of clarity, direction, and remarkable (bounce-back) power. When all note concentrations conclude, the blessings of brokenness flow without interruption.

Perfumista(s): Hagar (Genesis 16, 21), Rizbah (2 Samuel 21), Dinah (Genesis 34), Levite's concubine (Judges 19), Tamar (2 Samuel 13)

Scent of a Desperate Woman

Review: So good to the flesh, but so bad for the spirit. Seemingly good intentions hit the top notes, but as those notes fade, the heart is kindled in a silky aromatic slow burn of temporary fulfillment, adding to the base note, an increasing insatiable void of hunger and thirst.

Perfumista(s): Potiphar's Wife (Genesis 39), Rebekah, (Genesis 27), Sarah (Genesis 16)

Sound Mind

Review: Sound mind is tranquil in nature, beaming a breath of fresh air. One of the signature fragrances of Christ, it is light but powerful, with an aromatic essence of peace at its base. The heart of trusting in

God in all that you do acts as a lavender calming effect, inviting one to engage in a realm uninterrupted beauty sleep, a true rest in the Lord. It also beckons the wearer to a peace that surpasses all understanding in the midst anxiousness and the most dire circumstances.

Perfumista(s): Esther (Book of Esther), Jehosheba (2 Chronicles 22), Queen Vashti (Esther 1)

Virtuous Woman

Review: In one word...classic. A phenomenal scent for every woman's fragrance wardrobe! Fearfully and wonderfully made, top notes allure simple sophistication, while softened heart notes of selflessness, grace, and honor make this fragrance a standout. Virtuous Woman: a pleasing balance of dignity, poise, mystery, and faith. The empowering base essence of this aroma is Jesus, accompanied by a hint of elegance. Praised and priced far above rubies, a woman who fragrances herself with this scent is known to turn heads, changing the atmosphere in every place without saying a word.

Perfumista(s): Lydia (Acts 16), Mary the Mother of Jesus (Luke 1), Proverbs 31 Woman

Wisdom

Review: The most supreme and exquisite of all fragrances. It is topped with a reverential fear of the Lord. Wisdom is encompassed with a mature blend of earthy and eternal undertones. This fragrance is a divine composition of original vintage, showcasing common sense that brings health to the body. Wisdom is the principal thing! Tree-of-life heart notes empower the wearer to build up and establish herself and others with knowledge. The base of this lovely scent is understanding. It must be applied to every area of your life. Benefits of this aroma help the wearer to keep the path of righteousness, discretion, and honor, finding favor in the sight of God and man. It encourages one to talk less and listen more, learning from the experience of others. Perfumista(s): Bathsheba (2 Samuel 11), Naomi (Book of Ruth), Queen of Sheba (1 Kings 10)

Worship

Review: Heavenly! Worship is the ultimate aromatic indulgence for any believer. It is the most intimate of all fragrances. It is sweet communion with the Lord. Usually preceded by praise, this signature fragrance of Christ is beautifully accented by top notes of spirit and truth. As the top notes climax, soft, yielding notes of pure adoration are released in oneness with the Father.

Perfumista(s): Mary of Bethany (Mark 14), Anna (Luke 2)

Final Thoughts

I'm going to leave a bit of essential oil my late Grandma Smith and Grandma Dear left with me. No matter what situation I presented them with, one powerful drop from their Perfumed Letters has always resonated with me. Somewhere in the midst of conversation they would say, "Keep on living." I never fully understood they what meant then, but thank God for the wisdom in it revealed to me today.

You know how when you are doing everything you know how to do, living right unto Christ the best you know how by the leading of the Holy Spirit, crucifying the flesh--dying to your old ways and perhaps even falling but getting back up every now and again...? One day you glance over and the enemy flaunts a person(s) puppeted by his spirit strings, who appears to be more blessed, getting ahead and receiving the upper hand, seemingly happy and smiling, not thinking about Christ or consequence...and yet here you are being pressed on one hand and extracted by another. You get the feeling God has left and forgotten you, and now you are basically pissed off because the enemy is rejoicing and you are not. Ooohhh, I know exactly how you feel! It's like God, how could You let that happen and I'm over here trying. I know You see it. I have been there when days and nights do not feel like a Hallelujah and Glory to His name. I've had those exact thoughts, except I included a few expletives conversely with the Lord.

The enemy can sneak up and make a Perfumed Letter feel like she is missing out or that she does not have the upper hand, but I have encouraging news for the Concretes, Absolutes, and Essential Oils. To every Daughter of Christ, this is a shout-out: When the enemy comes in like a flood, the Lord will lift up a standard against him! What is that standard? As my late grandmothers would say, "Keep on living." Apostle Paul tells us in Philippians 1:21 NIV: "For to me, to live is Christ and to die is gain. If I am to go on living in the body, this will mean fruitful labor for me. Yet what shall I choose? I do not know!" When you don't know and you are confused as to how in the world the enemy is getting over, making you appear foolish, sarcastically mocking you with "Where is your God?" and it seems like the laborious process of the pressing and extraction of your perfume isn't recognized by Him, God tells you to choose life (Deuteronomy 30:19) and keep on living.

You have your Bible ready? Don't just take my word for it. Read Psalm 37 as it breaks this down further.

To note: When this passage of scripture mentions the wicked, it is not referring to the context of a witch, spells, and a broomstick. It is the translation of the Hebrew word "rasha," meaning ungodly (i.e. those who are spirited by the enemy that flaunts in your face, laughs at your defeat, those who molest your love and are without repentance, and who are condemned; those that believe in the life they live, they do not need God).

So what does it mean when God lifts up the standard against the enemy by your decision to keep on living? It means:

- the big chests and egos of the enemy will be deflated
- you will be rewarded and justified by doing right
- don't worry about the enemy's seeming success (mind your own business)
- keep on living and hope, and because you hope, you will inherit your land
- the wicked have a set time to "be" and then they disappear
- keep on living and you will have peace and enjoy it, and prosperity
- the Lord is laughing at them because He knows their day is coming; they will get theirs because God will trouble your trouble
- keep on living and let them be foolish, for what they had in store to destroy you and what they did to hurt you, they themselves will fall by it and be broken in heart
- what little power the enemy had in people or possessions will be broken
- keep on living and the Lord will hold you up
- keep on living and the Lord will care for you
- keep on living and your inheritance will endure forever (among your generations and kingdoms)
- keep on living and you will have plenty when famine comes
- the Lord's enemies who fragrance themselves with Pretty Pretender will be consumed (if they aren't for the Lord, they are against Him)
- keep on living and the Lord will direct your steps
- keep on living for when you fall, the Lord will uphold you
- keep on living and you will never be forsaken
- keep on living and your children won't have to beg for anything
- keep on living and your children will be a blessing
- you will dwell in your land forever (not borrowed, not rented, or leased, but you will live in your own land)

- you will see wrongdoers destroyed and their offspring perish
- keep on living and you speak wisdom and justice
- keep on living and you will not be condemned
- the Lord will exalt you
- keep on living and when the wicked are destroyed, God will grant you VIP seating to see it come to pass
- keep on living and while the wicked seem like they are flourishing, they will pass away
- a beautiful future is awaiting your arrival
- keep on living for there will be no future for the wicked
- keep on living for when you happen to get into trouble, the Lord will be your stronghold
- keep on living and He will deliver you

As a Perfumed Letter, I encourage you to keep on living and rock your perfume because the kingdom is inside of you. By this fragrant oil, your house is built by God, and by understanding it is established. "Through knowledge its rooms are filled with rare and beautiful treasures." (Proverbs 24:4, NIV). Keep on living for the descendants and nations that will come forth from your womb, cradled by you with the signature fragrances of Christ and the anointing in your perfume. Choose life and keep on living--for the Perfumed Letter you are, they will read, and know as life in Christ.

All things considered, your perfume is your anointing. The signature fragrances of Christ equip you for that anointing. What are you good at? What is that spiritual gift and or talent that comes naturally to you? Whatever it is, it was given to you by God. The skills and talents that you have are not by accident. They are given to you by God on purpose, for the purpose of His glory. Where is your heart? Wherever your heart is, there your treasure will be also. God put something in you that ONLY YOU can do best, out of the seven billion people in the world. Who or what is stopping you? God isn't.

Don't make excuses due to finances, marital status, education level, body shape, or even your residential area. It is of no consequence if you live in the hood or suburbia. Nothing shall by any means hurt you, so you have no excuse. Your pressing is not in vain. It cost Jesus His life, and quality is going to cost you something. Fine perfume is not cheap. Not everyone can afford your quality, and that's okay. If they want the clearance rack, off-brand synthetic copy, let them have it. Plant that seed, pray for them, and keep it moving.

You have been fragranced with every spiritual blessing. Everything that you need, God has already put inside of you. Girlfriend, don't limit yourself. With God, all things are possible. Let me emphasize to you, our Father has given you signature fragrances and a perfume especially made for you to be a blessing to someone else. Update your fragrance wardrobe if need be, and keep on living. It's not a question of whether you can, or if He can. The question is: Do you believe? You are softly perfumed in the love of His Spirit. You are written in His heart…you are God's Perfumed Letter.

About the Author

Robin Smith is a native of Cahokia, Illinois. She is a freelance writer and Editor-in-Chief of *Perfumed Ink*, an online magazine for the Christian woman. She is currently in her 12th year of active duty service in the United States Air Force. A graduate of Cahokia High School, Robin is pursuing a Bachelor of Arts degree in English with Ashford University. In addition to motherhood, duty, and education, she is pursuing certification as an Etiquette Instructor in St. Louis, Missouri. A bit of an adrenaline junkie, when she is not writing, she is involved in traveling, hiking, archery, and indoor rock climbing.

References

Copyright: www.Biblos.com,:
From 7004. qetoreth
from Strong's Concordance
"qetoreth: smoke, odor of (burning) sacrifice, incense
Original Word: ק ט □ ' ,ר ת ,
Part of Speech: Noun Feminine
Transliteration: qetoreth
Phonetic Spelling: (ket-o'-reth)
Short Definition: incense"

Feldman, M. (n.d.). Dr. Marc Feldman's Munchausen Syndrome, Malingering, Factitious Disorder, & Munchausen by Proxy Page. Dr. Marc Feldman's Munchausen Syndrome, Malingering, Factitious Disorder, & Munchausen by Proxy Page. Retrieved January 4, 2013, from http://www.munchausen.com

Patel, Parth N, Krupa M Patel, Dhaval S Chaudhary, Khushboo G Parmar, and Henil A Patel. "Extraction of Herbal Aroma Oils from Solid Surface." International Journal of Comprehensive Pharmacy 2.08 (2011): 1-10. www.pharmacie-globale.info. Web. 8 Jan. 2013.

CPSIA information can be obtained at www.ICGtesting.com
Printed in the USA
BVOW03s0749091013

333294BV00008B/398/P